WILDFLOWERS

of

DENALI
National Park

"DENALI"

Follow the rivers,
      explore some streams.
Stroll across tundra,
      through meadows and trees.
Climb up the mountains,
      traverse the scree.
Wander the ridges,
      watch bears run free.
Wide open spaces,
      most above all the trees.
Vast mountains, wide rivers
      ---- the Denali scene.

V.E.P.

DENALI NATIONAL PARK

Denali National Park had its beginning in 1906 when Charles Sheldon, a naturalist, studying Dall Sheep, determined that this was too great an area not to be preserved. He enlisted the aid of Judge James Wickersham, the Alaska Delegate to Congress, but early attempts to save it failed. Gold discoveries in the Kantishna Hills in 1905 prompted interest in the area. The urgency of the matter became apparent in 1915. Fairbanks and Nenana had started to grow and increasingly larger quantities of animals were being harvested for food.

It became a reality in 1917 but the name had been changed to McKinley National Park. Sheldon had preferred the name Denali which is the Athabascan Indian name for "great one or high one".

The Park was enlarged to the east in 1922 and to the west to include Wonder Lake in 1932. Road development started in 1922 and was completed to Wonder Lake in 1937. The road generally follows geological fault lines and caribou migration trails. Additional Park and Preserve lands were added to the west and north in 1980 including the historic mining district of Kantishna. At that time the name was changed to Denali National Park and Preserve.

Most topographic features are named after early explorers, geologists, pilots,or naturalists and by Sheldon during his visits from 1906 to 1908. Wonder Lake is an exception. As the story is told: Two early trappers happened upon the lake one day. One said to the other, "I wonder how we missed this one before." Eventually, it became known simply as Wonder Lake.

By studying the various books about the park, you will find that this magnificent country is as rich in history as it is in beauty.

WILDFLOWERS

of Denali National Park

Stony Creek
Lapland Rosebay

Verna E. Pratt
Frank G. Pratt

Alaskakrafts, Inc.
Post Office Box 210087
Anchorage, Alaska 99521-0087

First Printing

Library of Congress Catalog Card Number.......92-75672

ISBN 0-9623192-2-8

Printed in Japan by Dai Nippon Printing Co. Ltd.
through DNP (AMERICA), Inc.

All photographs are by Verna and Frank Pratt, unless otherwise credited.

Illustrations by Verna E. Pratt.

General Editor--Frank G. Pratt

Technical Editor--Verna E. Pratt

Cover Photos: Upper---Pink Plumes
Middle--Mount McKinley and Pasque Flower
Lower---Elegant Paintbrush and Frigid Arnica

DEDICATED

To our grand-daughter, Angelina, who, during the production of this book, spent many hours with us hiking on wet, spongy tundra, climbing mountains and crossing streams. Pleasures were many -- complaints few -- as we stopped many times for a photograph -- or two!

With energy, enthusiasm and excitement she observed -- bears running free and ground squirrels scampering by her feet. Denali offered the experience of watching nature unfold, tell stories and build memories that she can treasure forever. Such experiences with nature while young are sure to influence ones outlook on life in adult years. The great vast wilderness of Denali holds a wealth of knowledge and experience for young and old to enjoy and recall when the journey is over.

Angelina walking through a meadow of Eskimo Potato on the McKinley River Bar Trail in early July

ACKNOWLEDGEMENTS

Many thanks to all our friends and family members who graciously tolerated our busy schedule and lack of time for them while we were organizing this book.

Special Thanks to:

The U. S. Department of the Interior, National Park Service for granting our request for a Professional Photographer's Special Road Travel Permit. This allowed us to explore the Park much more easily and to establish more accurate lists in the limited time that we had available.

The owners and staff of Kantishna Roadhouse for their assistance that made exploring the west end of the Park much easier and more pleasant for us.

Steve Carwile, National Park Service, botanist at Denali National Park for assisting with proofreading and clarification of Park Rules and Regulations.

Amy Laverne Greeson of Anchorage for assisting with proofreading.

Tattler Creek

Polychrome Mt.

The authors exploring slopes in the backcountry

INTRODUCTION

The purpose of this book is to aid visitors to Denali National Park in recognition and better appreciation of the many wildflowers in the area. The diverse habitats that exist in the Park produce a wide range of plants that bloom from late May through August, when the fall color comes alive. The east end of the Park, near the George Parks Highway (except near lakes), is mostly dry and rocky. The flora here is similar to that of Interior and Northern Alaska. As you move westward, you progress through wet thickets, tundra, rocky slopes, alpine meadows and ridges, river bars and back to thickets, wet tundra and bogs, to Wonder Lake. If you travel on to the lodges at ''inholdings'' within the Park, you will go back to woodlands and river bars. Some of the flora in this part of the Park is similar to that of Southcentral Alaska. Much of the Park is above treeline, enabling the visitor to see many wonderful plants, from buses or on short walks, that would otherwise be available only to an avid hiker.

Blooming periods of some plants vary as much as 6 weeks, depending on severity of winter, time of snow melt, and elevation. Low elevation, exposed ridges and south-facing slopes will bloom earlier than deep valleys, north-facing and alpine slopes. Information on uses of plants is included in this book merely as points of interest and/or use in field survival situations. The identification and processing of any wild plant for use as food requires reasonable caution and attention to detail since, as indicated in the text, certain parts of some plants are totally unsuitable for use as food, and, in some instances, are even lethal. Personal allergies or sensitivities may also be cause for adverse reactions. Because attempts to use any wild plants for food depend on various factors controlled only by the reader, neither the author nor publisher assumes any responsibility for such adverse health effects as might be encountered in any individual case. Neither do we recommend gathering edible plants from the Park. The picking or gathering of any natural materials from the Park, with the exception of fungi and fruits (which includes berries) that are used for food, is strictly forbidden.

We sincerely hope that this book will inspire you to look more closely at the plants around you and enable you to more thoroughly enjoy your visit to this marvelous natural resource that is Denali National Park.

How to Use this Book

This book was arranged by color to make it easy to use. Some plants are difficult to place in this manner as their color varies and individual people see colors differently. Although some plants may readily be identified by a color photograph alone, it is strongly suggested that you also read the accompanying text for proper identification. Some species are very similar, and the new color films sometimes exaggerate certain colors. Other colors, especially delicate ones, do not always photograph well, and printed reproductions are not always completely accurate.

Descriptions in this book are as simple as possible--phrases are used rather than complete sentences. A set pattern is followed for ease in reading and similar plants are placed near each other. A glossary is provided for the more difficult terms. Both common and scientific names are given for each species where they are available. Not all plants have common names and some may be known by other names in different localities. Scientific names also change as further studies are made. We chose to use Eric Hultén's Flora of Alaska as our source for scientific names. (Note: Within the field of botany; however, current protocol is to not capitalize the species portion of the scientific name). Plant family names have since changed so we felt it best to follow the new nomenclature. Scientific names in parentheses indicate changes noted in Hultén's 1973 supplement to his Flora. Plant lists of different areas are included as an additional aid for more eager plant enthusiasts.

We noted plants visible from a moving vehicle (most visitors will see the Park by bus), explored around campgrounds, popular trails and took many back country hikes in an attempt to accurately list plants that may be found in the Park. There are surely many plants; however, that we have not yet seen as the Park covers some 6 million acres and some plants are found only in limited habitats. Many areas, that we visited, we saw only once during the flowering season and some plants are very difficult to see when not in bloom. Plant size will vary depending on elevation, moisture and type of soil. Although some plants shown are not common in other parts of Alaska, most can be seen elsewhere in the State.

Whether you hike the mountains or ride the bus there are many beautiful sights to see and uncountable opportunities to gather memories that will enrich your appreciation of the wonder that is --------- Denali.

TABLE OF CONTENTS

INTRODUCED PLANTS

Introduced plants are usually found around civilization. Most that we saw were near the Railroad Station and Park Entrance, and a few at Kantishna. Most had not become a problem, but we suspect that the Common Dandelion may someday pose a threat to the native flora as they are spreading beyond Savage River area. Their large leaves and aggressive spreading habit quickly crowd out small plants. See pages 42 and 79 for native dandelions.

Common Plantain

Shepherd's Purse

Knotweed

Pineapple Weed

Tansy Mustard

Squirrel Tail Grass

Clover

Common Dandelion

BLUE AND VIOLET-FLOWERED PLANTS

Meadow, Stony Dome
Bluebells, Bear Flower, Black-tipped Groundsel, Pink Plumes and Louseworts

Glaucous Gentian (Mt. Healy)

GLAUCOUS GENTIAN

Gentiana glauca

(Gentian / Gentianaceae)

Rocky tundra ~~~ Mid-June to late July ~~~ **Plant:** Perennial, 2 to 5" ~~~ Thick, stiff, stems, may be dark ~~~ **Leaves:** Opposite, thick, round, clustered near base, yellowish-green ~~~ **Flowers:** 2/3 to 3/4", tubular, green to teal-blue, upright in clusters.

FOUR-PARTED GENTIAN

Gentiana propingua

(Gentian / Gentianaceae)

Sandy, open areas ~~~ Late June to mid-July ~~~ **Plant:** Annual, 4 to 12", stems stiff ~~~ **Leaves:** Long, oval, pointed, rosette at base when young, opposite on branched stems, often dark at base ~~~ **Flowers:** 1/2 to 1" narrow, tubular, rosy lavender, upright in clusters.

MOSS GENTIAN

Gentiana prostrata

(Gentian / Gentianaceae)

Wet, open ground and scree ~~~ Mid-June to August ~~~ **Plant:** Small, sprawling, probably an annual, stems whitish ~~~ **Leaves:** Small, opposite, oval, light green ~~~ **Flowers:** Small, 1/4 to 1/3", bright blue, with white center, 4 or 5 petals, opens only in bright sunshine, often closes if shaded or touched.

Moss Gentian (Savage River)

Four-parted Gentian

FEW-FLOWERED CORYDALIS

Corydalis pauciflora

(Earthsmoke / Fumariaceae)

Wet alpine meadows ~~~ Mid-June to mid-July ~~~ **Plant:** Delicate perennial, 3 to 6" ~~~ **Leaves:** Blue-green, long-stemmed, basal, 3-lobed further divided into blunt segments ~~~ **Flowers:** 3/4 to 1" tubular with curved spur, bluish-violet with white throat, occasionally pink or white, 3 or 4 per stem.

Few-flowered Corydalis (Quigley Ridge)

Purple Cress (Quigley Ridge)

PURPLE CRESS

Cardamine purpurea

(Mustard / Brassicaceae)

Wet tundra and meadows ~~~ June through July ~~~ **Plant:** Small perennial, 3 to 5" ~~~ **Leaves:** Glabrous, dark green, pinnately divided ~~~ **Flowers:** 4 petals, about 1/4", lavender, pinkish or white, clustered at end of branches ~~~ **Fruit:** Long, narrow seed capsules.

SMELOWSKIA BOREALIS

Smelowskia borealis

(Mustard / Brassicaceae)

High alpine scree and talus ~~~ Late June to mid-July ~~~ **Plant:** Perennial rosette ~~~ **Flowers:** Very small, 4 petals, white to lavender, on 5 to 8" upright stems that quickly sprawl on the ground ~~~ **Fruit:** Long, twisted seed capsules, 4 varieties in the area with minor differences ~~~ **Comments:** *Smelowskia pyriformis* is very rare, endangered, very similar to *S. borealis* but flowers are white to cream-colored, and seed capsules are pear-shaped. None of the smelowskias are plentiful, and viewing requires hiking on scree and talus slopes. See page 125 for young rosette stage.

Smeloskia borealis (Thoro Ridge)

Alpine Forget-me-not (Highway Pass)

Mountain Forget-me-not (Cathedral Mt.)

Splendid Forget-me-not (Mt. Healy)

ALPINE FORGET-ME-NOT

Myosotis alpestris

(Borage / Boraginaceae)

Mountain meadows ～～ Late June to late July ～～ **Plant:** Perennial, 5 to 12" ～～ **Leaves:** 3/4 to 1-1/2", pointed, long, narrow, oval, bluish-green, alternate, hairy ～～ **Flowers:** 5 connected petals, salverform, sky blue (occasionally pink or white), 1/4 to 1/3" with a white inner ring and yellow center ～～ The Alaska State Flower.

MOUNTAIN FORGET-ME NOT

Eritrichium aretioides

(Borage / Boraginaceae)

High alpine in loose moist scree, occasionally tundra ～～ Mid-June to early July ～～ **Plant:** Perennial, small mounds ～～ **Leaves:** In rosettes, small, roundish, hairy and bluish-green ～～ **Flowers:** On short stems elongating to 3", bright blue, 5-petaled, salverform, with dark yellow eye. Also see page 125 ～～ **Comments:** Not very plentiful.

SPLENDID FORGET-ME-NOT

Eritrichium splendens

(Borage / Boraginaceae)

Dry, sandy areas near tree line ～～ Mid-June to early July ～～ **Plant:** Perennial in mounds ～～ **Leaves:** Very narrow, hairy, bluish-green, 3/4 to 1-1/2" long ～～ **Flowers:** 5-petaled, bright blue, salverform with bright yellow eye, on stems up to 3" long ～～ **Comments:** Seen only on Mt. Healy, east side.

BLUEBELLS, CHIMING BELLS

Mertensia paniculata

(Borage / Boraginaceae)

Woods, meadows ~~~ Mid-June to early August ~~~ **Plant:** Perennial to 22" ~~~ **Leaves:** Large, hairy, dark bluish-green, broad at base, tapering to a point, stem leaves alternate & narrower ~~~ **Flowers:** 5 joined petals in bell shape, pink in bud, later blue (occasionally pink or white)~~~ **Uses:** Edible flowers and leaves. See also page 1.

WILD GERANIUM

Geranium erianthum

(Geranium / Geraniaceae)

Woods, meadows ~~~ Mid-June to early August ~~~ **Plant:** Perennial, 14 to 24" ~~~ **Leaves:** 3 to 5-lobed, dissected, slightly hairy, veins obvious, reddish along edges when young, reddish-orange in fall ~~~ **Flowers:** Large, rosy-lavender (rarely white), 5 petals ~~~ **Fruit:** Long, beak-like, 5-parted, reflexed and curled.

MOUNTAIN HAREBELL

Campanula lasiocarpa

(Bluebell / Campanulaceae)

Rocky, stable alpine areas ~~~ July to early August ~~~ **Plant:** Small perennial basal rosette, 2 to 4" ~~~ **Leaves:** Oval, pointed, with shallow teeth; stem leaves small and alternate ~~~ **Flowers:** Violet-blue, upright, bell-shaped, 1 to 1-1/2" ~~~ **Comments:** One-flowered Harebell, *Campanula uniflora*, is a closely related plant with narrower leaves and narrow bell-shaped, bluish flowers that usually nod. Not plentiful or obvious where found.

Bluebells, Chiming Bells (Highway Pass)

Wild Geranium (West of Mt. Eielson)

Mt. Harebell (Mt. Healy)

One-flowered Harebell (Mt. Healy)

Monkshood (Mt. Healy)

MONKSHOOD

Aconitum delphinifolium ssp. *delphinifolium*

(Buttercup / Ranunculaceae)

Moist woods, meadows ～～ Late June through July ～～ **Plant:** Perennial, 10 to 30" ～～ **Leaves:** Deeply toothed, 3 to 5-lobed, divided to middle ～～ **Flowers:** Dark blue ～～ **Comments:** A similar plant is Dwarf Monkshood, *Aconitum delphinifolium* ssp. *paradoxum*, which may be found on rocky slopes, it is smaller, usually 1-flowered, and has broader leaf sections. The fruit is a 3-parted, upright seed capsule. Caution: Poisonous if eaten.

LARKSPUR

Delphinium glaucum

(Buttercup / Ranunculaceae)

Moist woods, alpine meadows ～～ Late June to early August ～～ **Plant:** Perennial, 2 to 5', stems purplish at first ～～ **Leaves:** Alternate, palmate, 3 to 5 deeply toothed pointed lobes ～～ **Flowers:** 3/4 to 1", dark bluish-purple, petals joined to form a spur. Flower stems mostly glabrous ～～ **Fruit:** Upright 3-parted seed capsule. Poisonous if eaten.

DWARF LARKSPUR

Delphinium brachycentrum

(Buttercup / Ranunculaceae)

Alpine scree slopes ～～ Mid-July to mid-August ～～ **Plant:** Perennial up to 15" (usually 4 to 8") ～～ **Lower leaves:** More rounded in outline than Tall Larkspur ～～ **Flowers:** White to royal blue, flower stems hairy. **Comments:** Not often seen, but plentiful in its habitat. Poisonous if eaten.

Larkspur (Roadside near Mt. Margaret)

Dwarf Larkspur (Backcountry, Polychrome Mt.)

PASQUE FLOWER, SPRING CROCUS

Pulsatilla patens

(Buttercup / Ranunculaceae)

Well drained, sandy soil ~~~ May to early June ~~~ **Plant:** Perennial up to 16", densely hairy when young ~~~ **Leaves:** Basal leaves purplish at first, very narrow divisions, appearing after the flowers ~~~ **Flowers:** Large, 2 to 2-1/2", violet, with 5 to 7 hairy tipped sepals with an obvious circle of bracts surrounding the stem below the flowers. ~~~ **Fruit:** Seed heads large, spirally twisted, see page 117 ~~~ **Comments:** *Anemone multiceps* is much smaller but similar in appearance. Flowers about 1". Leaves small, sections broader and less numerous. Fruit rounded, fluffing out at maturity. Poisonous if eaten.

Pasque Flower (Mt. Healy)

TALL JACOB'S LADDER

Polemonium acutiflorum

(Phlox / Polemoniaceae)

Moist tundra, meadows and thickets ~~~ Late June to mid-August ~~~ **Plant:** Perennial, 1 to 3', may be smaller in alpine, stems hairy ~~~ **Leaves:** Few, basal with petioles, smooth, 7 to 11 small pointed leaflets, stem leaves are few and sessile ~~~ **Flowers:** Lavender-blue with white center, up to 1", 5-pointed petals, calyx hairy and sticky ~~~ **Comments:** 1) Northern Jacob's Ladder, *P. boreale* ssp. *villosissimum*, can be seen on steep scree slopes in the back country in the Eielson / Polychrome area. The whole plant, which is about 5" tall, is densely hairy. Flowers are lavender to white, blooming in July and August. 2) Beautiful Jacob's Ladder, *P. pulcherrimum*, occurs ocassionally in dry alpine areas at the east end of the Park.

Anemone multiceps (Mt. Healy)

Northern Jacob's Ladder (Polychrome Mt.)

Tall Jacob's Ladder (Highway Pass)

Erigeron hyperboreus (Mt. Healy)

Siberian Aster (Riley Creek)

Saussurea angustifolia (Savage River)

ERIGERON HYPERBOREUS

Erigeron hyperboreus

(Aster / Asteraceae)

Gravelly and rocky areas in the mountains ～～ Late June through July ～～ **Plant:** Perennial, 3 to 5" ～～ **Leaves:** Narrow, spatulate, hairy ～～ **Flowers:** 3/4 to 1", ray flowers bluish-lavender fading to pinkish (sometimes white) ～～ **Comments:** Not plentiful, seen only once on Mt. Healy, northeast side.

SIBERIAN ASTER

Aster sibiricus

(Aster / Asteraceae)

Woods, meadows, into alpine ～～ Mid-June to early August ～～ **Plant:** Perennial up to 14", root spreader ～～ **Leaves:** Hairy, alternate, oblong, pointed, with a few teeth ～～ **Flowers:** Large, rosy-lavender with yellow centers ～～ **Fruit:** Tan fluffy seed head ～～ **Comments:** *Erigeron grandiflora* is a similar, smaller alpine plant from a simple tap root, ray flowers narrower, flowers pink to lavender.

SAUSSUREA ANGUSTIFOLIA

Saussurea angustifolia

(Aster / Asteraceae)

Tundra, wet meadows ～～ July and August ～～ **Plant:** Perennial, 6 to 14" ～～ **Leaves:** Alternate, long, narrow ～～ **Flowers:** Lavender, in thistle-like heads, grouped at top of stems ～～ **Comments:** *Saussurea viscida* is a similar low perennial found on moist tundra and scree. Leaves are in a hairy rosette, broad, elliptical, pointed with wavy edges. Flowers lavender in tight clusters in center of rosette. Blooming in July and August.

Saussurea viscida (Backcountry, Polychrome Mt.)

ALPINE VERONICA

Veronica wormskjoldii

(Figwort / Scrophulariaceae)

Alpine meadows ~~~ July to early August ~~~ **Plant:** Perennial up to 10" ~~~ **Leaves:** Uppermost are opposite, elongated oval, hairy ~~~ **Flowers:** Bluish-lavender, 5 petals (looks like 4, as top 2 are fused together and appear as one broad petal).

ALASKA SYNTHYRIS, KITTEN TAILS

Synthyris borealis

(Figwort / Scrophulariaceae)

High alpine ridges and tundra ~~~ Late May to mid-June ~~~ **Plant:** Perennial, hairy, small, 4 to 5" ~~~ **Leaves:** Lower are up to 1-1/4", rounded in outline, short stems, blunt teeth, somewhat lobed; upper are wedge-shaped with shallow teeth ~~~ **Flowers:** Blue, 5 petals in tight elongated

WEASEL SNOUT

Lagotis glauca ssp. *minor*

(Figwort / Scrophulariaceae)

Wet, rocky mountainous areas ~~~ June ~~~ **Plant:** Perennial, 5 to 8" ~~~ **Leaves:** 2 or 3 basal with petioles, lanceolate, serrated, 2 to 4", smooth; stem leaves much smaller, shorter and sessile ~~~ **Flowers:** Very small, in terminal cylindrical spike, blue or white.

Alpine Veronica (Stony Dome)

Weasel Snout (Backcountry, Thoro Ridge)

Alaska Synthris (Backcountry, Mt. Galen)

Pendant Pod Oxytrope (Mt. Healy)

PENDANT POD OXYTROPE

Oxytropis deflexa ssp. *foliolosa*
(Pea / Fabaceae)

Dry, gravelly areas ~~~ June ~~~ **Plant:** Perennial, 6 to 12" ~~~ **Leaves:** Many flat, oval, pointed, hairy leaflets on stiff upright stems ~~~ **Flowers:** Many, very small, bluish-lavender ~~~ **Fruit:** Pod, slightly hairy, hanging downward.

MERTEN'S OXYTROPE

Oxytropis mertensiana
(Pea / Fabaceae)

Gravelly areas in the mountains ~~~ Late June to mid-July ~~~ **Plant:** 2 to 3", sprawling ~~~ **Leaves:** Having 1 to 3 (rarely 5) pointed leaflets, mostly glabrous, with hairs around the edges ~~~ **Flowers:** 1 to 3, purplish (rarely white), calyx black with hairs ~~~ **Fruit:** Erect pod, black hairs, slightly curved ~~~ **Comments:** Not plentiful, seen only on Mt. Galen.

Merten's Oxytrope (Mt. Galen)

PURPLE OXYTROPE, BLACKISH OXYTROPE

Oxytropis nigrescens
(Pea / Fabaceae)

Rocky alpine ridges and dry, open, exposed areas on tundra ~~~ June ~~~ **Plant:** Perennial, flat on ground ~~~ **Leaves:** Short with many small hairy leaflets ~~~ **Flowers:** Purple to blue (occasionally white), usually 2 per stem, calyx covered with black (occasionally white) hairs ~~~ **Fruit:** Seed pod with short beak up to 1-1/2" long, gray to black hairs, lying flat on the ground ~~~ **Comments:** Scamman's Oxytrope, *Oxytropis scammaniana*, is similar, but flowers are more bluish, frequently 3 per stem, are on upright stems, and pods are short and thick. See also page 140.

Purple Oxytrope (Eielson Visitor Center)

Purple Oxytrope seed pod (Eielson V. C.)

MELANDRIUM APETALUM

Melandrium apetalum

(Pink / Caryophyllaceae)

Dry, grassy slopes and rocky outcrops in mountains ~~~ June ~~~ **Plant:** Perennial, up to 6" ~~~ **Leaves:** Basal, opposite on stems, narrow, slightly hairy ~~~ **Flowers:** Nodding, lavender, protruding slightly from the swollen, sticky calyx, usually one per stem ~~~ **Fruit:** Capsule, upright when mature, seeds large, light brown with broad wing ~~~ **Comments:** *Melandrium macrospermum* is similar but with upright flowers, 1 to 3 per stem, seeds grayish-brown with thick wing.

ALPINE MILK VETCH

Astragalus alpinus

(Pea / Fabaceae)

Gravelly areas, open areas, up into alpine ~~~ Mid-June to late-July ~~~ **Plant:** Perennial, up to 8", usually sprawling ~~~ **Leaves:** Many leaflets, slightly hairy beneath, oblong to pointed ~~~ **Flowers:** Tight cluster, lavender to blue and white ~~~ **Fruit:** Pod, reflexed, with black hairs, groove down back side.

ARCTIC LUPINE

Lupinus arcticus

(Pea / Fabaceae)

Meadows, fields ~~~ Mid-June to late July ~~~ **Plant:** Up to 8" ~~~ **Leaves:** On long stems, like spokes of umbrella, leaflets 5 to 10, oval and pointed ~~~ **Flowers:** Medium to dark blue (rarely white), on long thick spike ~~~ **Fruit:** Seed pod, hairy, probably poisonous if eaten ~~~ **Comments:** Nootka Lupine, *Lupinus nootkatensis*, is similar but taller with short leaf stems, most leaves on flowering stem, flowers usually more rosy and lighter. ~~~Hybrids occur.

Melandrium apetalum (Savage River)

Alpine Milk Vetch (Cathedral Mt.)

Arctic Lupine (West of Eielson Visitor Center)

Selkirk's Violet (Mt. Healy)

SELKIRK'S VIOLET

Viola selkirkii
(Violet / Violaceae)

Woods rich with humus, frequently near alders ～～ Late May to mid-June ～～ **Plant:** Small perennial ～～ **Leaves:** Light green, in loose clump, long-stemmed, heart-shaped, pointed, shallow teeth, deep sinus ～～ **Flowers:** One, small, rosy-lavender, with white center ～～ **Fruit:** 3-parted seed capsule ～～ **Uses:** Edible flowers and leaves ～～ **Comments:** Not plentiful, seen only on Mt. Healy.

MARSH VIOLET

Viola epipsela
(Violet / Violaceae)

Streams, moist woodlands, meadows ～～ June ～～ **Plant:** Perennial, 2 to 4" ～～ **Leaves:** Heart-shaped, 5/8 to 3/4" (becoming larger and more rounded), small teeth, on 2" stems (elongating in age) ～～ **Flowers:** Few, small, light lavender ～～ **Fruit:** 3-parted seed capsule opening flat ～～ **Uses:** Plant edible cooked or raw ～～ **Comments:** Alaska Violet, *Viola langsdorfii*, might be found in alpine meadows. A taller plant with larger violet to purple (rather square-looking) flowers.

Marsh Violet (Fairbanks, AK)

BOG VIOLET

Pinguicula villosa
(Bladderwort / Lentibulariaceae)

Marshy areas at low elevations ～～ Late June to late July ～～ **Plant:** Perennial, insectivorous ～～ **Leaves:** In rosette, yellowish-green, edges rolled upwards, sticky ～～ **Flowers:** Small, bluish-violet, with spur, on 2 to 3" hairy stem ～～ **Comments:** Seen only on McKinley River Bar Trail, but abundant there.

Bog Violet (McKinley Bar Trail)

PINK-FLOWERED PLANTS

Mt. Healy from George Parks Highway
Wild Sweet Pea

Prickly Rose (Riley Creek)

PRICKLY ROSE

Rosa acicularis

(Rose / Rosaceae)

Fields, margins of woods and open slopes ~~~ Mid-June to early July ~~~ **Shrub:** Up to 4 feet tall with many prickles ~~~ **Leaves:** With stipules and usually having 5 toothed leaflets ~~~ **Flowers:** 2 to 3" with 5 rounded petals that are velvety on top side, silky on the back, sepals persistent and attached to the fruit ~~~ **Fruit:** Oval, with pocket of seeds in middle, soft when ripe, usually dark red ~~~ **Uses:** Good for jellies, jams. Seeds should be removed. Petals used for teas and jellies. Very high in vitamin C. Leaves also used for teas.

Rose Hip (Triple Lakes Trail)

NAGOONBERRY

Rubus arctica

(Rose / Rosaceae)

Bogs, meadows, edges of woods up into alpine ~~~ Mid-June to early July ~~~ **Plant:** Perennial, 3 to 6", underground runners ~~~ **Leaves:** Long stemmed with 3 leaflets, toothed and coarse-veined ~~~ **Flowers:** Pink, 1", with 5 to 8 narrow petals ~~~ **Fruit:** Aggregate (like a raspberry) ~~~ **Uses:** Edible raw or cooked, excellent flavor, but not very plentiful.

Nagoonberry (Polychrome Mt.)

Nagoonberry fruit (Anchorage)

CUCKOO FLOWER

Cardamine pratensis

(Mustard / Brassicaceae)

Wet areas usually at low elevations ~~~ June to early July ~~~ **Plant:** Perennial, 6 to 10" tall ~~~ **Leaves:** Few, basal, glabrous, pinnately divided, see below, stem leaves shorter ~~~ **Flowers:** 3/8 to 5/8", pale pink, 4 petals ~~~ **Fruit:** Seed pod, narrow, 1-1/2 to 2" long ~~~ **Comments:** A similar plant with smaller white flowers is *Cardamine umbellata.*

Cuckoo Flower (Kantishna)

PARRY'S WALLFLOWER

Parrya nudicaulis ssp. *interior*

(Mustard / Brassicaceae)

Moist slopes and tundra ~~~ Early June to mid-July ~~~ **Plant:** Perennial, up to 10" with very long root ~~~ **Leaves:** Basal, minutely hairy, 2 to 4", dark green, lanceolate, pointed, usually with wavy edge ~~~ **Flowers:** 1/2 to 1", pink, white or lavender, 4 petals, aromatic ~~~ **Fruit:** Long, pointed pod swollen around seeds (2 to 4 per pod) ~~~ **Uses:** Leaves edible raw or cooked, root edible if cooked. See also page 140.

Parry's Wallflower (Highway Pass)

PALLAS WALLFLOWER

Erysimum pallasii

(Mustard / Brassicaceae)

Dry, gravelly, rocky slopes ~~~ Early to mid-June ~~~ **Plant:** Perennial, 2 to 6" tall, thick tap root, small clump ~~~ **Leaves:** Bluish-green, mostly basal, lanceolate, somewhat rounded, shallow teeth, hairy ~~~ **Flowers:** 1/4 to 1/3", pink, 4 petals, clustered close to the leaves at first ~~~ **Fruit:** Very long narrow seed pod, upright, curved ~~~ **Comments:** Not plentiful, seen only in Polychrome area.

Pallas Wallflower (West of Polychrome Pass)

Gorman's Douglasia (Backcountry, Mt. Healy)

GORMAN'S DOUGLASIA

Douglasia gormanii
(Primrose / Primulaceae)

Rocky areas in the mountains ~~~ Late May to early June ~~~ **Plant:** Perennial, dense cushion often with old dead leaves attached ~~~ **Leaves:** 1/4 to 1/3", narrow, fine branched hairs on top side ~~~ **Flowers:** 1/4 to 1/3", on short stems, petals connected at base, salverform.

CHUKCHI PRIMROSE

Primula tschuktschorum ssp. *arctica*

[*Primula eximia*--Hultén's 1973]

(Primrose / Primulaceae)

Very wet alpine meadows ~~~ Late May through June ~~~ **Plant:** Perennial, 4 to 6", stem often has white coating ~~~ **Leaves:** 2 to 3-1/2" long, broad, spatulate, toothed, rounded at end ~~~ **Flowers:** Bright pink, 5 pointed petals united at base, salverform, calyx of 5 sepals united (cone-shaped) ~~~ **Comments:** Seen only on Mt. Galen, Thoro Ridge and Primrose Ridge.

Chukchi Primrose (Primrose Ridge)

PIXIE EYE PRIMROSE, WEDGE LEAF PRIMROSE

Primula cuneifolia

(Primrose / Primulaceae)

Rocky alpine areas ~~~ Late May to late June ~~~ **Plant:** Small perennial, 1 to 3" ~~~ **Leaves:** Rosette, light green, toothed, wedge-shaped ~~~ **Flowers:** Pink (occasionally white) with yellow eye, 5 petals joined at base, rounded and indented at end. **Comments:** Not plentiful in the Park. Seen only on Quigley Ridge, Wickersham Dome, Mt. Galen and Thorofare Pass.

Pixie-eye Primrose (Wickersham Dome)

FRIGID SHOOTING STAR

Dodecatheon frigidum

(Primrose / Primulaceae)

Meadows, wet tundra and alpine slopes ~~~ June to mid-July ~~~ **Plant:** Perennial to 10" ~~~ **Leaves:** Basal with stems, spade-shaped, light green, wavy edges ~~~ **Flowers:** Magenta with white ring next to stamens, petals connected and reflexed, 2 to 5 in umbel ~~~ **Fruit:** Upright cylindrical capsule, see below.

Frigid Shooting Star (Highway Pass)

ALASKA SPRING BEAUTY

Claytonia sarmentosa

(Purslane / Portulacaceae)

Wet, rocky slopes, meadows and tundra ~~~ Mid-June to mid-August ~~~ **Plant:** Perennial, weak succulent stem, up to 4" ~~~ **Leaves:** Fleshy, light green, basal (few) are long-stemmed and spoon-shaped, flower stems have 2 opposite, sessile leaves ~~~ **Flowers:** 5 delicately rounded petals, white to light pink with darker stripes, calyx of 2 sepals ~~~ **Uses:** Whole plant is edible raw or cooked ~~~ **Comments:** Apparently not plentiful in the Park.

Alaska Spring Beauty (Stony Dome)

SCAMMAN'S SPRING BEAUTY

Claytonia scammaniana

(Purslane / Portulacaceae)

Alpine scree ~~~ Mid-June to early-August ~~~ **Plant:** Clump to 2-1/2" ~~~ **Leaves:** Many, small, narrow, reddish and fleshy ~~~ **Flowers:** Bright pink with darker veins, 5 rounded petals, calyx of 2 sepals ~~~ **Uses:** Whole plant edible raw or cooked. See also pages 128 and 131.

Scamman's Spring Beauty (Thoro Ridge)

Tall Fireweed (Savage River)

TALL FIREWEED

Epilobium angustifolium

(Evening Primrose / Onagraceae)

Dry open areas, hillsides, roadsides and meadows ～～ Mid-June to mid-August ～～ **Plant:** Erect perennial from deep horizontal roots, up to 4', sometimes branched ～～ **Leaves:** Alternate on flowering stems, sessile, dark green above, lighter below, veins prominent, up to 6", broad at base tapering to a narrow point, leaves turn orange-red or purplish in the fall ～～ **Flowers:** Magenta (sometimes light-pink or white), 3/4 to 1-1/2", 4 rounded petals (top 2 slightly smaller), 4 long narrow purplish sepals, stigma forms a cross ～～ **Fruit:** Long narrow capsule releasing tiny seeds with fine fluff (carried by wind) ～～ **Uses:** New reddish spring shoots are edible, jelly and honey can be made from flowers ～～ **Comments:** There are many Willow Herbs (Epilobium sp.) in Alaska. Flowers are very small, white or pink. Plants slender and usually in wet areas, near creeks or alpine meadows. Apparently not common in the Park.

Willow Herb sp.
(WickershamDome)

DWARF FIREWEED, RIVER BEAUTY

Epilobium latifolium

(Evening Primrose / Onagraceae)

Gravelly areas along rivers and up into alpine ～～ Late June through mid-August ～～ **Plant:** Up to 20" perennial from horizontal roots ～～ **Leaves:** Sessile, alternate on flowering stems, bluish-green, somewhat fleshy appearance, elliptical ～～ **Flowers:** 1 to 2", 4 large equal, oval and pointed, magenta (occasionally pale pink or white) petals, 4 narrow purplish sepals, lower flowers blooming first, stigma forms a cross ～～ **Fruit:** Long, narrow capsule releasing tiny seeds with fine fluff (carried by wind).

Dwarf Fireweed (Tattler Creek)

WOOLLY LOUSEWORT

Pedicularis kanei
[*Pedicularis lanata*---Hultén 1973]
(Figwort / Scrophulariaceae)

Dry stony tundra ~~~ Late May to late June ~~~ **Plant:** Perennial, up to 10", long tap root, thick stem, covered with woolly white hairs when young ~~~ **Leaves:** Basal with long stems, alternate on stem, finely pinnate with toothed leaflets, purplish when young ~~~ **Flowers:** Pink, hood beakless ~~~ **Uses:** Root edible raw or cooked ~~~ **Comments:** 1) Arctic Lousewort, *P. langsdorfii*, is similar but has sparsely hairy leaves with broad central rib. Flowers have a hood with beak and are light pink to lavender. Blooms June to mid-July. 2) Whorled Leaf Lousewort, *P. verticillata*, 8 to 14" plant with a loose basal rosette of slightly hairy leaves. Flowers are grouped just above whorls of leaves around the stem. Blooms July and August in meadows. 3) Fern Leaf Lousewort, *P. sudetica* ssp. *interior*, 6 to 16" plant with a loose rosette. Leaves are glabrous. Flowers are rose to wine-colored. Found in wet meadows in mid-July to mid-August.

Woolly Lousewort (Wickersham Dome)

Whorled-leaf Lousewort (Stony Dome)

Arctic Lousewort (Backcountry, Mt. Healy)

Fern leaf Lousewort (Stony Dome)

Elegant Paintbrush (Highway Pass)

ELEGANT PAINTBRUSH

Castilleja elegans

(Figwort / Scrophulariaceae)

Rocky soil in open areas ~~~ Late June to early August ~~~ **Plant:** Perennial, 3 to 15", very variable both in growth form and color, one to many hairy flowering stalks (sometimes branched) ~~~ **Leaves:** Alternate on stems, narrow, uppermost leaves often divided, upper leaves and bracts usually rosy-colored (sometimes light-yellow to cream-colored) ~~~ **Flowers:** About 1" long, inconspicuous, between hairy bracts, upper lobe green, lower lobe purplish and 1/2 the length of upper lobe.

Moss Campion (Polychrome Pass)

MOSS CAMPION

Silene acaulis ssp. *acaulis*

(Pink / Caryophyllaceae)

Gravelly slopes in alpine areas and gravelly stream beds ~~~ Early June to mid-July ~~~ **Plant:** Perennial, cushion plant with long tap root ~~~ **Leaves:** Small, short, flat, narrow, bright green in dense mats ~~~ **Flowers:** Salverform with very short stems, pink (rarely white or lavender. One green specimen found near Sable Mt.), very aromatic ~~~ **Comments:** *Silene acaulis* ssp. *subacaulescens* is similar but with longer flower stems and narrower leaves.

Pale Corydalis (Visitor Access Center)

PALE CORYDALIS

Corydalis sempervirens

(Earthsmoke / Fumariaceae)

Loose, rocky or disturbed ground at low elevations ~~~ Mid-June to late July ~~~ **Plant:** Annual or biennial, branched, up to 30" ~~~ **Leaves:** Alternate, light bluish-green, 3 to 5-lobed, divided again into blunt segments ~~~ **Flowers:** Small, pink with yellow tips at end of branches ~~~ **Fruit:** Long, narrow seed capsule.

LAPLAND ROSEBAY

Rhododendron lapponicum

(Heath / Ericaceae)

Stony, damp or dry slopes ~~~ June ~~~ **Shrub:** 4 to 14" ~~~ **Leaves:** Small, oval, evergreen, thick, clustered at ends of branches, upper surface medium to dark green and dull, lower surface lighter with rusty resin dots ~~~ **Flowers:** Cup-shaped, 3/8 to 5/8", magenta, with pronounced stigma. Calyx of 5 small triangular sepals, resin dotted, hairs along edges. See also page iii.

Lapland Rosebay (Thoro Ridge)

ALPINE AZALEA

Loiseleuria procumbens

(Heath / Ericaceae)

Dry alpine ridges and rocky areas in the tundra ~~~ Late May to mid-June ~~~ **Shrub:** Sprawling on ground ~~~ **Leaves:** Hard, evergreen, very small, oval, usually dark green ~~~ **Flowers:** Many, very small, light pink, cup-shaped, nearly covering the shrub when in full bloom.

BOG BLUEBERRY

Vaccinium uliginosum

(Heath / Ericaceae)

Bogs, woods, tundra up into alpine ~~~ Late May to mid-June ~~~ **Shrub:** 4 to 20" ~~~ **Leaves:** 1/2 to 3/4", alternate, oval, dark green, turning orange to red in fall ~~~ **Flowers:** Pink, bell-shaped, hanging under branches ~~~ **Fruit:** 1/2", round to oval, dark blue, acidic berry, ripe in late June to early September ~~~ **Uses:** Berry-jellies , pies, and breads. Leaves and berries-teas. A favorite edible of the bears. See also page 122.

Alpine Azalea (Wickersham Dome)

Bog Blueberry (Railroad Depot)

Bog Blueberry (Wickersham Dome)

Low-bush Cranberry (near Park entrance)

L0W-BUSH CRANBERRY, LINGONBERRY, MOUNTAIN CRANBERRY

Vaccinium vitis-idaea
(Heath / Ericaceae)

Bogs, woods, mountain slopes into alpine ~~~ June to mid-July ~~~ **Shrub:** 1 to 8" from horizontal roots ~~~ **Leaves:** Alternate on stems, evergreen, shiny, oval, hard, edges rolled under ~~~ **Flowers:** Bell-shaped, pink to white, at ends of branches ~~~ **Fruit:** Round maroon berry, ripens in late August to September ~~~ **Uses:** Jam, jelly breads, desserts, tea. See also page 122.

Low-bush Cranberry (near Park entrance)

KINNIKINNICK, MEAL BERRY

Arctostaphylos uva-ursi
(Heath / Ericaceae)

Dry, open areas and hillsides ~~~ Late May to mid-June ~~~ **Shrub:** Mat-forming, from long tap root, sprawling with long branches ~~~ **Leaves:** Rounded, spatulate, evergreen, thick, leathery. Smooth dark green above, rough and lighter below ~~~ **Flowers:** Pinkish-white, urn-shaped at ends of branches ~~~ **Fruit:** Round, dull red, mealy, tasteless berry. Previous years berries frequently visible when flowering.

Kinnikinnick (Mt. Healy)

Kinnikinnick (Teklanika)

PURPLE MT. SAXIFRAGE, FRENCH KNOT PLANT

Saxifraga oppositifolia

(Saxifrage / Saxifragaceae)

Moist, rock outcroppings, crevices and scree up into alpine ~~~ May and June ~~~ **Plant:** Perennial, sprawling, long fibrous root system ~~~ **Leaves:** Dark green, very small in rosettes ~~~ **Flowers:** Magenta, 1/2", cup-shaped, turning purplish after maturity ~~~ **Fruit:** 2-parted, erect seed capsules. See also page 128.

BOG ROSEMARY

Andromeda polifolia

(Heath / Ericaceae)

Bogs ~~~ June ~~~ **Shrub:** up to 8" ~~~ **Leaves:** Evergreen, hard, grayish-green above, lighter and bluish beneath, narrow, up to 1" long, edges rolled under ~~~ **Flowers:** Urn-shaped, pink, clustered at top of branches on pink stems ~~~ **Uses:** Caution---poisonous!

BOG CRANBERRY

Oxycoccus microcarpus

(Heath / Ericaceae)

Bogs ~~~ June ~~~ **Shrub:** Trailing ~~~ **Leaves:** Very small, oval, evergreen, alternate, dark green, hard ~~~ **Flowers:** 5 reflexed petals, very small, light pink, on curved 1 to 1-3/4" stem ~~~ **Fruit:** Oval maroon berry, lying on the ground, ripening in late August or September ~~~ **Uses:** Jellies, jams, breads.

Purple Mt. Saxifrage (Tattler Creek, Sable Mt. Trail)

Bog Rosemary (Wonder Lake Ranger Station)

Bog Cranberry (Wonder Lake Ranger Station)

Bog Cranberry (Wonder Lake Ranger Station)

Pink Pyrola (Park entrance)

PINK PYROLA

Pyrola asarifolia

(Wintergreen / Pyrolaceae)

Woods, mountainsides, thickets ～～ Mid-June to mid-July ～～ **Plant:** Perennial with pinkish stem, up to 12" ～～ **Leaves:** Evergreen, basal with stems, rounded, waxy, soft, 1 to 2" ～～ **Flowers:** 5 rounded petals, cup-like, 1/2 to 5/8", mostly facing downwards on a thick stiff stem, long protruding style ～～ **Fruit:** 5-parted, round capsules also with protruding style.

SMALL-FLOWERED PYROLA

Pyrola minor

(Wintergreen / Pyrolaceae)

Mountainsides, alpine meadows ～～ Late June to early August ～～ **Plant:** Perennial, up to 6" ～～ **Leaves:** Basal, 2 or 3, small, 1/2 to 3/4", round, evergreen ～～ **Flowers:** 1/4 to 1/2", pale pink, bell-like, facing downwards ～～ **Fruit:** 5-parted round capsule with protruding stigma.

Small-flowered Pyrola
(Stony Dome)

Twin Flower (Wickersham Dome)

TWIN FLOWER

Linnaea borealis

(Honeysuckle / Caprifoliaceae)

Woods, alpine slopes ～～ Mid-June to early August ～～ **Shrub:** Trailing, evergreen～～ **Leaves:** Ovate, 1/2" long, toothed at the end, yellowish-green, lighter below ～～～**Flowers:** On leafy 2-1/2 to 3" stem, pink and white, funnel-shaped, aromatic.

PINK PLUMES

Polygonum bistorta

(Buckwheat / Polygonaceae)

Alpine meadows and wet tundra ～～ Mid-June to mid-July ～～ **Plant:** Perennial, 6 to 10", long horizontal rhizome ～～ **Leaves:** 4 to 5", lanceolate, pointed, dark green above, lighter below ～～ **Flowers:** Pink, cup-shaped, very small, on tight 2" spike ～～ **Uses:** Leaves edible raw or cooked.

Pink Plumes (Stony Dome)

ESKIMO POTATO

Hedysarum alpinum

(Pea / Fabaceae)

Rocky or gravelly areas from river bars to alpine ～～ Late June through July ～～ **Plant:** Perennial, 12 to 18" branched stem, long horizontal root ～～ **Leaves:** 15 to 20 leaflets having strong mid-vein and obvious side veins on underside ～～ **Flowers:** Long raceme of 10 to 40 small, narrow, pink flowers, 1/2 to 2/3" long, see also page v ～～ **Fruit:** Seed pods with round section with transverse veins, see below ～～ **Uses:** Root is edible if cooked. A favorite food of bears ～～～ **Comments:** *Hedysarum hedysaroides* is a smaller alpine plant without side branches. Flowers few, magenta to purple.

Eskimo Potato (Highway Pass)

WILD SWEET PEA

Hedysarum mackenzii

(Pea / Fabaceae)

Low elevations ～～ June ～～ **Plant:** Clumping ～～ **Leaflets:** Showing mostly only a strong mid-vein ～～ **Flowers:** Large, aromatic, clustered at end of stems ～～ **Fruit:** Seed pod with horizontal veins, see below ～～ **Comments:** Reportedly poisonous.

Wild Sweet Pea (Toklat River)

Sticky Oxytrope (Cathedral Mt.)

STICKY OXYTROPE

Oxytropis viscida

(Pea / Fabaceae)

Dry, rocky areas ～～ June to early July ～～ **Plant:** Perennial, 6 to 10", clump, thick branched tap root ～～ **Leaves:** Upright, many, with many leaflets, stipules light-colored with narrow points ～～ **Flowers:** Purplish-pink (sometimes bluish), clustered at end of stem, calyx and stem hairy and sticky ～～ **Fruit:** Short upright pod, black, hairy, with short straight beak.

NOOTKA MILK VETCH

Astragalus nutzotinensis

(Pea / Fabaceae)

River bars and gravelly soil in the mountains ～～ Mid-June to mid-July ～～ **Plant:** Perennial, on root runner, weak sprawling ～～ **Leaves:** 7 to 15 oval or pointed leaflets ～～ **Flowers:** 2 to 4, rosy-purple (pink at base), calyx has black hairs ～～ **Fruit:** Long pod, reddish, lying on ground, straight at first then semicircular ～～ **Comments:** Polar Milk Vetch, *Astragalus polaris*, is similar but with 1 or 2 flowers. Leaflets may be cuneate at tip. Pods elliptical, see below.

Nootka Milk Vetch (Cathedral Mt.)

Nootka Milk Vetch (Polychrome Mt.)

Polar Milk Vetch seed pod (Stony Dome)

YELLOW-FLOWERED PLANTS

Highway Pass
Arctic Poppy

CAPITATE LOUSEWORT

Capitate Lousewort (Mt. Galen)

Pedicularis capitata

(Figwort / Scrophulariaceae)

Alpine slopes, tundra ~~~ Early June to mid-July ~~~ **Plant:** Perennial, 3 to 4", on horizontal roots ~~~ **Leaves:** Long-stemmed,singular along roots, 2 to 2-1/2", pinnate and toothed ~~~ **Flowers:** 3 to 4 at end of hairy stem, light yellow to pinkish with tinge of brown on tip of hood ~~~ **Comments:** A favorite food of arctic ground squirrels.

Arctic ground squirrel gathering lousewort flowers

OEDER'S LOUSEWORT

Oeder's Lousewort (Mt. Galen)

Pedicularis oederi

(Figwort / Scrophulariaceae)

Wet areas in alpine and on tundra ~~~ Mid-June through July ~~~ **Plant:** Perennial, thick stem, up to 7" ~~~ **Leaves:** Glabrous, mostly basal, pinnate with fine indentations ~~~ **Flowers:** Bright yellow in dense thick spike, elongating in age, tip of hood brownish-red.

LABRADOR LOUSEWORT

Labrador Lousewort (Riley Creek)

Pedicularis labradorica

(Figwort / Scrophulariaceae)

Bogs, woods, alpine and tundra ~~~ Late June to late July ~~~ **Plant:** Short-lived perennial, branched, up to 14" ~~~ **Leaves:** Small, on stems, pinnate with shallow, fine teeth ~~~ **Flowers:** Small, light yellow with brownish hood, scattered near end of branches. This branched plant is obvious even in seed.

YELLOW PAINTBRUSH

Castilleja caudata

(Figwort / Scrophulariaceae)

Roadsides, fields, meadows, along streams ~~~ Late June to early August ~~~ **Plant:** Perennial, 10 to 14" ~~~ **Leaves:** Hairy, long, narrow ~~~>**Flowers:** Small (upper lip greenish-yellow, lower lip yellow), tucked into colorful light yellow or cream-colored entire bracts (a few upper ones may be split), lower bracts and stems may turn reddish in age.

Yellow Paintbrush (Near Park entrance)

Maydell's Oxytrope (Wickersham Dome)

MAYDELL'S OXYTROPE

Oxytropis maydelliana

(Pea / Fabaceae)

Stony slopes and tundra ~~~ June to early July ~~~ **Plant:** 4 to 5" perennial clump ~~~ **Leaves:** Hairy, pinnately divided, old stipules (around base of plant) reddish-brown ~~~ **Flowers:** Several, clustered at ends of branches, calyx hairy ~~~ **Fruit:** Pod, elliptical with long bent beak ~~~ **Comments:** Most oxytropes are poisonous.

Hairy Arctic Milk Vetch (Highway Pass)

HAIRY ARCTIC MILK VETCH

Astragalus umbellatus

(Pea / Fabaceae)

Rocky slopes, moist tundra ~~~ Mid-June to late July ~~~ **Plant:** Perennial from horizontal roots, up to 6" ~~~ **Leaves:** Alternate on stem, pinnately divided, hairy beneath ~~~ **Flowers:** Small, clustered at top of stems, calyx hairy ~~~ **Fruit:** Pod, pointed at both ends, covered with black hairs.

Barnacle Saxifrage (Savage River)

CILIATE SAXIFRAGE, CUSHION SAXIFRAGE, [BARNACLE SAXIFRAGE]

Saxifraga eschscholtzii
(Saxifrage / Saxifragaceae)

Usually high alpine, in rocky outcroppings, lichen tundra ~~~ Late May and June ~~~ **Plant:** Perennial, small rounded cushions with long root ~~~ **Leaves:** Very small, light grayish, hairs along edges, in very tight rosettes ~~~ **Flowers:** Very small, on very short stems, petals yellow ~~~ **Fruit:** Red, 2-parted, spreading seed capsule ~~~ **Comments:** Common name in brackets is name given by the author.

Spider Plant (Mt. Galen)

SPIDER PLANT

Saxifraga flagellaris
(Saxifrage / Saxifragaceae)

Rocky places in high alpine ~~~ Late June to late July ~~~ **Plant:** Perennial, fibrous roots, red runners bearing new plants ~~~ **Leaves:** Oval, in dense rosette, coarse hairs along edges, alternate on flowering stem ~~~ **Flowers:** 1/2 to 5/8", few, clustered at top of 2 to 3" stem.

THYME-LEAF SAXIFRAGE

Saxifraga serpyllifolia
(Saxifrage / Saxifragaceae)

High, dry, rocky places in mountains ~~~ mid-June to late July ~~~ **Plant:** Perennial, fibrous roots, very small ~~~ **Leaves:** Oval, shiny, very small, in tight rosettes, few small alternate on flowering stems ~~~ **Flowers:** 1/2", bright yellow with orange spots, on 2 to 3" stem.

Thyme-leaf Saxifrage (Thoro Ridge)

BOG SAXIFRAGE

Saxifraga hirculus

(Saxifrage / Saxifragaceae)

Bogs, meadows and wet tundra ~~~ Late June through July ~~~ **Plant:** Perennial clump, up to 8", fibrous roots ~~~ **Leaves:** Matted, small, narrow, smooth, alternate on hairy flower stems ~~~ **Flowers:** Up to 3/4", usually 1 or 2 per stem, calyx of 5 sepals with hairs along edges, reflexing early ~~~ **Fruit:** 2-pronged seed capsule.

YELLOW SPOTTED SAXIFRAGE

Saxifraga bronchialis

(Saxifrage / Saxifragaceae)

Rocky areas in the mountains ~~~ Mid-June to late July~~~ **Plant:** Perennial clump, fibrous roots, ~~~ **Leaves:** Smal, pointed, oval, fine hairs along edges, in tight rosettes,  small and alternate on flowering stems ~~~ **Flowers:** 3/8 to 1/2", cup-shaped, light yellow with bright yellow spots, clustered at ends of 3 to 5" stems.

Bog Saxifrage (Roadside bog)

Yellow Spotted Saxifrage (Mt. Healy)

SMALL YELLOW VIOLET

Viola biflora

(Violet / Violaceae)

Mountain slopes, especially damp scree ~~~ Mid-June through July ~~~ **Plant:** Loose perennial, sprawling on ground ~~~ **Leaves:** Few, rounded to kidney-shaped, small, light green ~~~ **Flowers:** Small, elongated, bright, usually 2 per stem ~~~ **Fruit:** 3-parted seed capsule opening flat. The only yellow violet in the area ~~~ **Uses:** Edible flowers and leaves.

Small Yellow Violet (Polychrome Pass)

Dwarf Buttercup (Stony Dome)

DWARF BUTTERCUP

Ranunculus pygmaeus

(Buttercup / Ranunculaceae)

Late snow beds in mountains ~~~ Mid-July to early August ~~~ **Plant:** Perennial, very small ~~~ **Leaves:** Basal, deeply divided into 3 to 5 lobes with blunt segments ~~~ **Flowers:** Singular, petals very small (as long as sepals), domed seed head obvious at flowering time ~~~ **Comments:** Arctic Buttercup or Creeping Buttercup, *Ranunculus hyperboreus*, has similar leaves but is a creeping plant in muddy areas at lower elevations, it has 3 or 4 small petals and 3 or 4 sepals. Common on Triple Lakes Trail. All buttercups are poisonous if eaten.

Creeping Buttercup (Wasilla)
Photo-Forrest Baldwin

SNOW BUTTERCUP

Ranunculus nivalis

(Buttercup / Ranunculaceae)

Late snow beds, mountain streams ~~~ Early June to early August ~~~ **Plant:** Perennial, up to 5" ~~~ **Leaves:** One or two, basal, 3-lobed with blunt segments, glabrous, stem leaves 3 to 5-segmented ~~~ **Flowers:** Singular, 5 shiny petals, calyx of 5 sepals covered with black hairs ~~~ **Comments:** Mountain Buttercup, *Ranunculus eschscholtzii*, is less common in the Park. It is similar, but grows in clumps. Sepals have light-colored hairs and it has more flowers per stem. All buttercups are poisonous if eaten.

Snow Buttercup (Sable Mt. Trail)

Mountain Buttercup (Mt. Galen)

RANUNCULUS GELIDUS

Ranunculus gelidus

(Buttercup / Ranunculaceae)

Wet scree slopes and talus ~~ June ~~ **Plant:** Sprawling perennial, spreading fibrous roots ~~ **Leaves:** Glabrous, 3 deep lobes with additional narrow, rounded segments ~~ **Flowers:** One to three on 2 to 3" stem, petals longer than sepals ~~ **Comments:** All buttercups are poisonous if eaten.

Ranunculus gelidus (Thoro Ridge)

LAPLAND BUTTERCUP

Ranunculus lapponicus

(Buttercup / Ranunculaceae)

Bogs, wet acidic woodlands ~~ June to mid-July ~~ **Plant:** Creeping perennial, from horizontal roots ~~ **Leaves:** Long thin stems, 3 broad deeply-divided lobes (middle lobe with about 5 blunt teeth, side lobes again divided and lobed) ~~ **Flowers:** Singular, on long thin stems, light yellow, 6 to 8 narrow petals slightly longer than sepals, calyx of 3 sepals ~~ **Seed head:** See drawing ~~ **Comments:** Poisonous if eaten. Seen along Horseshoe Lake Trail.

Lapland Buttercup (Wasilla)
Photo-Forrest Baldwin

YELLOW ANEMONE

Anemone richardsonii

(Buttercup / Ranunculaceae)

Moist woods, meadows and thickets ~~ Late May to late July ~~ **Plant:** Perennial, on thin horizontal root ~~ **Leaves:** Long-stemmed, 3 broad lobes, again divided with shallow teeth ~~ **Flowers:** No petals, 5 to 7 pointed yellow sepals (brownish on underside) on 3 to 6" erect stem having a circle of bracts below flower ~~ **Comments:** Poisonous if eaten.

Yellow Anemone (Stony Dome)

Marsh Marigold (Pond near Polychrome Pass)

MARSH MARIGOLD

Caltha palustris ssp. *arctica*

(Buttercup / Ranunculaceae)

In water or very wet areas, usually slow moving water ～～ June ～～ **Plant:** Perennial with hollow stems ～～ **Leaves:** 1-1/4 to 2-1/2", shallowly toothed, thick, round to kidney-shaped, usually just above the water ～～ **Flowers:** 5 bright yellow sepals, greenish on underside, clustered at the end of hollow stems just above the water ～～ **Comments:** Poisonous if eaten raw. Edible if cooked.

Yellow Dryas (Stony Creek)

YELLOW DRYAS

Dryas drummondii

(Rose / Rosaceae)

Dry, gravelly areas at low elevations and on river bars ～～ June to early July ～～ **Shrub:** Low, mat-forming ground cover ～～ **Leaves:** Leathery, coarse-veined, basal, oval, serrated edges, greenish-brown above, whitish from hairs beneath ～～ **Flowers:** 5 petals, yellow, nodding on 3 to 4" whitish stem, calyx covered with brownish hairs ～～ **Fruit:** Twisted at first, see above; then tan and fluffy, somewhat like a dandelion.

Yellow Dryas (Toklat River)

Yellow Dryas (Thorofare River)

SIBBALDIA PROCUMBENS

Sibbaldia procumbens

(Rose / Rosaceae)

Rocky alpine slopes ～～ Late June and July ～～ **Plant:** Perennial with thick woody base, up to 2" extending to 3 or 4" in seed, dead leaves prominent at base ～～ **Leaves:** Blue-green, 3-lobed, wedge-shaped, with 3 to 7 teeth at ends ～～ **Flowers:** Very small, 5 light yellow petals which are smaller than sepals.

Sibbaldia procumbens (Stony Dome)

POTENTILLA BIFLORA

Potentilla biflora

(Rose / Rosaceae)

Rocky slopes ～～ Mid-June to mid-July ～～ **Plant:** Perennial with woody base, up to 8" ～～ **Leaves:** Somewhat hairy, stiff, divided to middle with narrow segments ～～ **Flowers:** Usually 2 per stem, about 3/4", petals indented and longer than sepals.

Potentilla biflora (Wickersham Dome)

TUNDRA ROSE, SHRUBBY CINQUEFOIL

Potentilla fruiticosa

(Rose / Rosaceae)

Bogs, rocky and scree slopes ～～ Mid-June to early August ～～ **Shrub:** Up to 30", branches with peeling bark ～～ **Leaves:** Usually 5 narrow, bluish thick leaflets ～～ **Flowers:** About 1", rounded petals folded back, bracts on seed capsules very distinctive. See page 36.

Tundra Rose (Polychrome Mt.)

Tundra Rose (Polychrome Pass)

Hooker's Potentilla (Mt. Healy)

HOOKER'S POTENTILLA

Potentilla hookeriana

(Rose / Rosaceae)

Rocky areas ~~~ Late May through June ~~~ **Plant:** 8 to 10" branched stems with straight hairs ~~~ **Leaves:** 3-parted, coarse-looking, dark green above, white felt-like beneath ~~~ **Flowers:** Small, up to 1/2", petals slightly longer than sepals, slightly indented ~~~ **Comments:** *Potentilla hyparctica* is a similar, low-growing (up to 4") plant in alpine areas. Leaves only slightly hairy beneath. Flowers 5/8 to 3/4". Petals bright yellow, deeply indented.

Potentilla hyparctica (Mt. Galen)

ONE-FLOWERED CINQUEFOIL

Potentilla uniflora

(Rose / Rosaceae)

Rocky outcroppings ~~~ Early June to mid-July ~~~ **Plant:** Perennial, clump, 3 to 6", hairy stems ~~~ **Leaves:** Basal on hairy stems, 3-parted and shallowly toothed, underside densely hairy, edges silvery from hairs ~~~ **Flowers:** About 3/4", bright yellow, velvet-like, petals much longer than sepals with an orange blotch at base, indented at end, usually 1 per stem, see also page 140 ~~~ **Comments:** Villous Cinquefoil, *Potentilla villosa*, reportedly seen in the Park. Leaves are larger, darker green, very coarse-veined, and flowers are slightly larger.

One-flowered Cinquefoil (Quigley Ridge)

Villous Cinquefoil (Juneau, AK)

NORWEGIAN CINQUEFOIL

Potentilla norvegica ssp. *monspeliensis*

(Rose / Rosaceae)

Dry open areas ~~ July ~~ **Plant:** Branched perennial up to 15", young plants resemble strawberry plants ~~ **Leaves:** Few, basal, 3-parted and coarse-looking, toothed, on short stems, stem leaves alternate with stipules ~~ **Flowers:** Small, sepals longer than petals folding upward over seed capsules. See One-flowered Cinquefoil, page 36.

ROSS AVENS

Geum rossii

(Rose / Rosaceae)

Alpine meadows and slopes ~~ Early June to mid-July ~~ **Plant:** Perennial, clump, up to 12" ~~ **Leaves:** Mostly basal, 3 to 6", slightly hairy above, glabrous beneath, pinnately divided and toothed ~~ **Flowers:** Few, 1 to 1-1/4", clustered at ends of stems.

Norwegian Cinquefoil (McKinley River Bar Trail)

Ross Avens (Mt. Margaret)

LARGE LEAF AVENS

Geum macrophyllum ssp. *perincisum*

(Rose / Rosaceae)

Woods, meadows at low elevations ~~ Late June to early August ~~ **Plant:** Up to 2 feet, perennial, clump ~~ **Leaves:** Large, mostly basal, pinnately divided and toothed, hairy, coarse, end lobes broad and deeply lobed ~~ **Flowers:** Small, 1/2 to 5/8", light yellow ~~ **Fruit:** globular, bristly.

Large Leaf Avens (Kantishna)

Dwarf Arctic Butterweed (Sable Mt.)

Senecio atropurpureus (Highway Pass)

DWARF ARCTIC BUTTERWEED

Senecio residifolius

(Aster / Asteraceae)

Moist, gravelly alpine slopes ～～ July ～～ **Plant:** Perennial, often reddish, up to 4" ～～ **Leaves:** Mostly basal, reddish when young, lyrate to oval with shallow blunt teeth ～～ **Flowers:** 1", usually singular, disk flowers orange, ray flowers dark yellow and reddish on back.

SENECIO FUSCATUS

Senecio fuscatus

(Aster / Asteraceae)

Alpine meadows and moist scree ～～ July ～～ **Plant:** Perennial, up to 6", densely hairy when young ～～ **Leaves:** Hairy on both sides, basal leaves rounded to spatulate with slightly wavy edges, stem leaves smaller ～～ **Flowers:** 1 to 1-1/2", one or more, bright yellow ～～ **Comments:** Similar varieties are: 1) *S. atropurpureus* ssp. *tomentosa* with dark purplish stem when young, involucral bracts with purplish or brownish hairs, leaves mostly glabrous. 2) *S. atropurpureus* ssp. *frigidus*, similar to ssp. tomentosa but with very short ligulate flowers (appearing only partially in bloom) .

Senecio fuscatus (Thorofare Pass)

BLACK-TIPPED GROUNDSEL

Senecio lugens

(Aster / Asteraceae)

Bogs, roadsides, thickets and meadows ~~~ Late June to early August ~~~ **Plant:** Perennial, up to 2", stems are very dark early in the year ~~~ **Leaves:** Basal, glabrous, oval to oblong, slightly pointed with wavy edges, stem leaves long and narrow with minor indentations ~~~ **Flowers:** About 1", clustered at ends of stems, ray flowers very narrow, involucral bracts have black tips ~~~ **Comments:** 1) *S. pauperculus* is similar to the above, found in wet areas, basal leaves are smaller, and stem leaves toothed, no black tips on bracts. 2) *S. pauciflorus* is similar to *S. pauperculus*, but basal leaves are rounded, stem leaves deeply toothed.

Black-tipped Groundsel (Sanctuary River)

Senecio pauciflorus (Riley Creek)

Senecio pauperculus (Riley Creek)

Frigid Arnica (Polychrome Pass)

FRIGID ARNICA

Arnica frigida

(Aster / Asteraceae)

Dry, gravelly and rocky areas ~~~ June and July ~~~ **Plant:** Perennial, up to 12" ~~~ **Leaves:** Mostly glabrous, basal leaves are broad with stems, somewhat pointed, usually with wavy edges; stem leaves are sessile, usually entire, narrow and small ~~~ **Flowers:** Bright yellow, 2 to 3", usually single on a hairy stem, bracts sometimes purplish and hairy ~~~ **Fruit:** Seed with a few hairs, pappus white and barbellate, see above ~~~ **Comments:** Hoary marmots and arctic ground squirrels eat the flower heads. See also page 108.

ALPINE ARNICA

Arnica alpina ssp. *angustifolia*

(Aster / Asteraceae)

Near Park entrance, less common elsewhere ~~~ Mid-June to late July ~~~ **Plant:** Similar to Frigid Arnica ~~~ **Leaves:** Hairy, narrower and more pointed, bracts are hairy and glandular ~~~ **Seeds:** Densely hairy ~~~ **Comments:** Tall Alpine Arnica, *Arnica alpina* ssp. *attenuata,* is found near Park entrance, similar to Alpine Arnica but up to 22", with 3 to 5 flowers per stem.

Tall Alpine Arnica (Park entrance)

Alpine Arnica (Park entrance)

LESSING'S ARNICA

Arnica lessingii

(Aster / Asteraceae)

Meadows and rocky slopes ~~~ Mid-June to early August ~~~ **Plant:** Perennial, to 10" ~~~ **Leaves:** Mostly basal in a tight rosette, hairy above and along edges ~~~ **Flowers:** Solitary, nodding, light yellow, central disk flowers very loose, anthers and bracts purplish, very hairy ~~~ **Fruit:** Seed, glabrous to hairy with barbellate, light tan pappus.

Lessing's Arnica (Stony Dome)

ALPINE HAWK'S BEARD

Crepis nana

(Aster / Asteraceae)

Gravelly areas ~~~ Mid-June to mid-July ~~~ **Plant:** Biennial, cushion ~~~ **Leaves:** Ovate with long stems ~~~ **Flowers:** Very small, dandelion-like, on short, branched stems ~~~ **Fruit:** Small, dandelion-type seed heads ~~~ **Comments:** *Crepis elegans* is similar but up to 10" tall, leaves with longer stems and more teeth, flowers on longer stems.

Alpine Hawk's Beard (Backcountry, Polychrome Mt.)

Crepis elegans (Park entrance)

Alpine Hawk's Beard (Backcountry, Polychrome Mt.)

Northern Goldenrod (Mt. Healy)

NORTHERN GOLDENROD

Solidago multiradiata

(Aster / Asteraceae)

Meadows and rocky areas ~~~ Mid-June to August ~~~ **Plant:** Perennial, up to 18" with thick stiff stem ~~~ **Leaves:** Long, oblong, pointed, shallow teeth, becoming shorter upwards on the stem ~~~ **Flowers:** In dense clusters of small heads at top of stem ~~~ **Uses:** Teas and herbal baths, probably not an allergen as is commonly believed.

KAMCHATKA DANDELION

Taraxacum kamchaticum

(Aster / Asteraceae)

Rocky, alpine slopes and meadows ~~~ Mid-June to early August ~~~ **Plant:** Small perennial from tap root ~~~ **Leaves:** Purplish at base, 2 to 3", lobes triangular, end lobe blunt ~~~ **Seeds:** Mostly smooth ~~~ **Comments:** Other native dandelions in the area are: 1) Alaska Dandelion, *T. alaskanum*, similar to above but leaf lobes closer together and more pointed, seeds are smooth at base but rough in middle section ~~~ 2) *T. lacerum*, with deeply serrated leaves, flower stems are frequently purplish, involucral bracts have horns (small hooked protrusions at the ends), seeds have a long beak at the end (longer than the seed). ~~~ 3) *T. cerataphorum* (group) with broader irregular leaves ~~~ and 4) Pink Dandelion, *T. carneocoloratum*, with flesh-colored flowers. See page 79.

Kamchatka Dandelion (Tattler Creek)

Taraxacum lacerum (Back Country, Polychrome Mt.)

Alaska Dandelion (Stony Dome)

ARCTIC POPPY, LAPLAND POPPY

Papaver lapponicum

(Poppy / Papaveraceae)

Sandy, gravelly soil in mountains and on the tundra ～～ Mid-June to late July ～～ **Plant:** Perennial with long root, 6 to 10" hairy stem ～～ **Leaves:** Basal, hairy, lobed (lower segments divided again and separated slightly from other lobes --- see drawing) ～～ **Flowers:** Lemon yellow, 1 to 1-1/2", cup-shaped, 4 petals ～～ **Fruit:** Pear-shaped capsule (broadest at top), apparently a favorite of animals as they are frequently eaten off before maturity, see also page 27 ～～ **Comments:** Other poppies in the area are: 1) Macoun's Poppy, *P. macounii*, similar to Arctic Poppy, slightly taller, larger flowers, leaf stems long, lower sections of leaves not divided, capsule broadest at the middle; and 2) Alaska Poppy, *P. alaskanum*, similar to Macoun's Poppy but in a dense clump with many old leaf stems still attached, leaf stems very short, capsule short and broad, especially at top. 3) Pink Poppy, *P. alboroseum*, has reportedly been seen in the Park. It has very small pale pink flowers with yellow centers.

Arctic Poppy (Thoro Ridge)

Alaska Poppy (Backcountry, Mt. Healy)

Macoun's Poppy (Polychrome Mt.)

Draba aurea (Mt. Healy)

Draba stenoloba (Polychrome Rest Area)

DRABA AUREA

Draba aurea

(Mustard / Brassicaceae)

Dry, rocky areas ~~~ June ~~~ **Plant:** Usually branched, perennial, up to 12" ~~~ **Leaves:** Basal rosette when young, oval to spatulate, several on stems, grayish-green, hairy ~~~ **Flowers:** 4 petals, very small, clustered at ends of branches ~~~ **Fruit:** Long, hairy, capsule, sometimes twisted ~~~ **Comments:** Distinctive, as it is the only tall yellow draba in the area.

Alpine Draba (Polychrome Mt.)

DRABA STENOLOBA

Draba stenoloba

(Mustard / Brassicaceae)

Dry alpine areas ~~~ Mid to late June ~~~ **Plant:** 2 to 3", likely to be taller in other locations, probably a short-lived perennial ~~~ **Leaves:** Basal rosette, ovate to lanceolate, slightly wavy edges, dull green, hairy; stem leaves oval, slightly toothed and alternate ~~~ **Flowers:** Very small, pale yellow ~~~ **Fruit:** Long, narrow, glabrous, on a stem the same length or longer ~~~ **Comments:** Seen only at Polychrome Rest Area.

ALPINE DRABA

Draba alpina

(Mustard / Brassicaceae)

Gravelly or rocky areas in the mountains ~~~ June ~~~ **Plant:** Perennial clump from long tap root ~~~ **Leaves:** In tight clumps, oblong to lanceolate with branched hairs, straight hairs around edges ~~~ **Flowers:** Yellow, on 2 to 4" leafless stem with straight and branched hairs ~~~ **Fruit:** Glabrous, oblong capsule, pointed at end, see also opposite page. ~~~ **Comments:** *Draba macrocarpa* is a similar plant with hairs on seed capsules, stems can be glabrous or slightly hairy, these 2 species hybridize.

Alpine Draba

Draba macrocarpa

DRABA DENSIFOLIA

Draba densifolia

(Mustard / Brassicaceae)

Scree slopes ~~~ Early to mid-June ~~~ **Plant:** Very low, dense cushion ~~~ **Leaves:** Very small, mostly glabrous in very tight rosettes ~~~ **Flowers:** Small on short, leafless, mostly glabrous stems ~~~ **Fruit:** Ovate, hairy seed capsule ~~~ **Comments:** *Draba caesia*, a similar species, has hairy leaves in rosettes, flowers are smaller on hairy leafless stems, seed capsule is glabrous.

DRABA STENOPETALA

Draba stenopetala

(Mustard / Brassicaceae)

Loose, fine, gravelly slopes and rocky areas ~~~ Late May to early June ~~~ **Plant:** Small perennial, mat-forming, from long tap root ~~~ **Leaves:** In dense rosettes, very small, hairy spatulate ~~~ **Flowers:** Very small with 4 narrow petals ~~~ **Comments:** Distinctive because of narrow petals, but difficult to see when not in bloom as it is very small.

Alpine Draba (Polychrome Rest Area)

Draba densifolia (Thoro Ridge)

Draba stenopetala (Mt. Healy)

Thoroughwax (Mt. Healy)

Soapberry, male flowers

Soapberry, female flowers

THOROUGHWAX

Bupleurum triradiatum ssp. *arcticum*

(Parsley / Apiaceae)

Open, stony hillsides ~~~ Late June to early August ~~~ **Plant:** Up to 2 feet at low elevations, very short in alpine ~~~ **Leaves:** In clump at base, long, narrow, stiff, lily-like ~~~ **Flowers:** Very small, yellow (sometimes blotched with purple) in a double umbel ~~~ **Comments:** Distinctive as there are no other plants in the area with yellow umbel.

SOAP BERRY

Shepherdia canadensis

(Oleaster / Elaeagnaceae)

Gravelly river beds, woods and mountain slopes ~~~ Late May to mid-June ~~~ **Shrub:** 1 to 3 feet, greatly branched with rusty scales on new growth ~~~ **Leaves:** Oval, dark green above, light green below with rusty scales, new buds copper-colored from scales ~~~ **Flowers:** Very small, no petals, 4 yellow sepals, male and female on separate shrubs ~~~ **Fruit:** Bitter, edible, oval red berries (with scales) ~~~ **Uses:** Traditional use, whipped and sweetened as a dessert topping. A favorite food of bears.

Soapberry (Teklanika Campground)

WHITE AND CREAM-FLOWERED PLANTS

Highway Pass
Bear family feeding on Bear Flower

Alaska Spiraea (Savage River)

ALASKA SPIRAEA

Spiraea beauverdiana

(Rose / Rosaceae)

Woods, meadows and alpine slopes ~~~ Mid-June to mid-July ~~~ **Shrub:** With thin branches, 6 to 30" ~~~ **Leaves:** Alternate, oblong, toothed near the ends ~~~ **Flowers:** Very small, in flat-topped clusters, brown flat-topped seedheads remain on the shrub for more than one season ~~~ **Uses:** Leaves used for making teas.

Mountain Avens (Cathedral Mt.)

MOUNTAIN AVENS, 8-PETALED AVENS

Dryas octopetala

(Rose / Rosaceae)

Rocky alpine slopes ~~~ Mid-June to mid-July ~~~ **Sub-shrub:** Forming large mats ~~~ **Leaves:** Dark green above, whitish below, with wavy edges ~~~**Flowers:** 1" across, on 2 to 4" stems, usually 8 petals, usually tracking the sun ~~~ **Fruit:** Seed head, twisted at first, then whorled ~~~ **Uses:** A favorite food of sheep. See also pages 122 & 125. ~~~ **Comments:** Entire-leaf Avens, *Dryas integrifolia*, is similar a shrub but leaves have smooth edges and are shiny above (hybridization occurs). Found along river bars and gravelly areas usually at low elevations.

Entire-leaf Avens (Teklanika Campground)

Mountain Avens seed head (Thoro Ridge)

CLOUDBERRY, SALMONBERRY

Rubus chamaemorus

(Rose / Rosaceae)

Bogs, moist tundra ~~~ June ~~~ **Plant:** Perennial, up to 6", from creeping rootstock ~~~ **Leaves:** Coarsely veined, 5-lobed and toothed ~~~ **Flowers:** 4 or 5 petals, 3/4", white, male and female on separate plants ~~~ **Fruit:** Like a raspberry, light orange when ripe ~~~ **Uses:** May be eaten raw or cooked, fruit spoils quickly, makes excellent jelly, seeds are large ~~~ **Comments:** Traditionally called Salmonberry by Alaska Natives as berries look like a clump of salmon eggs. It is not to be confused with *Rubus spectabilis*, also called Salmonberry, which is found south of the Alaska Range and has pink flowers on tall biennial canes.

Cloudberry (Chugach Mts.,near Anchorage)

RASPBERRY

Rubus idaeus

(Rose / Rosaceae)

Edges of woods ~~~ June to early July ~~~ **Shrub:** Biennial canes, up to 4 feet with prickles ~~~ **Leaves:** 3 to 5 leaflets, toothed, heavily veined, whitish beneath ~~~ **Flowers:** 5/8", 5 petals ~~~ **Fruit:** Red berry ~~~ **Uses:** Raw, jelly, jam.

Cloudberry (Anchorage)

Raspberry (Morino Trail)

Raspberry (Anchorage)

Sitka Burnet (Highway Pass)

SITKA BURNET

Sanguisorba stipulata

(Rose / Rosaceae)

Woods, meadows and thickets ～～ Late June to late July ～～ **Plant:** Perennial, up to 20", from underground runners ～～ **Leaves:** Long-stemmed, pinnately divided, leaflets rounded and toothed ～～ **Flowers:** No petals, cylindrical spike, stamens pronounced ～～ **Uses:** Edible raw when young.

WILD RHUBARB

Polygonum alaskanum

(Buckwheat / Polygonaceae)

Open areas, low to mid elevations ～～ July ～～ **Plant:** Perennial, 2 to 5 feet, thick stem ～～ **Leaves:** Long, lanceolate, light green below, darker above, veins obvious ～～ **Flowers:** No petals, very aromatic, calyx creamy-white ～～ **Uses:** Edible raw or cooked, slightly acidic.

ALPINE MEADOW BISTORT

Polygonum viviparum

(Buckwheat / Polygonaceae)

Alpine meadows and slopes ～～ Mid-June to late July ～～ **Plant:** Perennial, 6 to 12" ～～**Leaves:** Long, narrow, dark green, smooth ～～ **Flowers:** Very small and dainty on long spike ～～ **Fruit:** Seed, often forming roots and leaves before dropping to the ground, see page 111 ～～ **Uses:** Leaves edible, favored by animals.

Wild Rhubarb (Kantishna)

Alpine Meadow Bistort (Savage River)

DEATH CAMAS, CAMAS WAND LILY

Zygadenus elegans

(Lily / Liliaceae)

Meadows and alpine slopes ~~~ July ~~~ **Plant:** Perennial, bulbous, 10 to 14", growing in a clump ~~~**Leaves:** Light grayish-green, long and narrow ~~~ **Flowers:** Creamy-white with green blotch at base ~~~**Comments:** Poisonous if eaten, the bulb looks similar to a wild onion.

ALP LILY

Lloydia serotina

(Lily / Liliaceae)

Rocky places in the alpine ~~~ June to early July ~~~ **Plant:** Small bulbous perennial up to 4" ~~~ **Leaves:** Few, fine, grass-like ~~~ **Flowers:** 6 tepals (petals and sepals that look the same), creamy-white with purple veins ~~~ **Fruit:** Round with 3 sections.

Death Camas (Highway Pass)

Alp Lily (Mt. Healy)

FALSE ASPHODEL

Tofieldia coccinea

(Lily / Liliaceae)

Dry, rocky places in alpine ~~~ June ~~~ **Plant:** Small perennial, up to 4" ~~~ **Leaves:** Narrow, sedge-like ~~~ **Flowers:** Very small in spike at end of stem with one small leaf. Petals can be tipped with pink. Ovary and anthers pinkish, very variable ~~~ **Comments:** *Tofieldia pusilla* is similar to above but grows in damp tundra, flowers are creamy-white on 3 to 6" leafless stem see page 135.

False Asphodel (Mt. Margaret)

Black Currant (Riley Creek)

NORTHERN BLACK CURRANT

Ribes hudsonianum

(Gooseberry / Grossulariaceae)

Moist woodlands ~~~ June ~~~ **Shrub:** Up to 30" ~~~ **Leaves:** Toothed, shallowly lobed, strong smelling, somewhat maple-shaped, turning yellow in fall ~~~ **Flowers:** Small, white, 5 petals, in upright clusters close to main stem ~~~ **Fruit:** Black, dull-looking, very sour berries in upright clusters ~~~ **Uses:** Edible, jelly, dye.

Black Currant (Triple Lakes Trail)

BERING SEA SPRING BEAUTY

Claytonia acutifolia

(Purslane / Portulacaceae)

Very wet places in mountains ~~~ July ~~~ **Plant:** Perennial with thick root ~~~ **Leaves:** Glabrous, long, narrow, stiff and pointed ~~~ **Flowers:** 5 rounded white petals with yellowish center, 2 sepals ~~~ **Comments:** Tuberous Spring Beauty, *Claytonia tuberosa*, is a slender perennial usually with one flowering stem having 2 short narrow leaves. It grows from a long thin underground stem and deep bulbous root.

Bering Sea Spring Beauty (Thoro Ridge)

Tuberous Spring Beauty (Thoro Ridge)

CAPITATE VALERIAN

Valeriana capitata

(Valerian / Valerianaceae)

Moist woods, thickets and meadows ~~~ Mid-June to late July ~~~**Plant:** Perennial, 8 to 12" ~~~ **Leaves:** Basal, oval and pointed on long stems, stem leaves are 3 to 5-parted and pointed~~~ **Flowers:** In dense rounded head, maroon in bud, becoming pink and then white.

CANADIAN DOGWOOD

Cornus canadensis

(Dogwood / Cornaceae)

Woods, tundra, low alpine ~~~ Mid-June to late July ~~~ **Plant:** 2 to 5" perennial on trailing rootstock ~~~ **Leaves:** Elliptical with arcuate veins, 4 or 5 in a whorl around stem, 2 smaller opposite leaves below (frequently withered) ~~~ **Flowers:** 4 white (occasionally green or pink) bracts (2 short and 2 long) with arcuate veins and sharp points, no petals, sepals are green ~~~ **Fruit:** A bunch of soft orange to red berries with white pulp ~~~ **Uses:** At one time berries were cooked and served as a pudding, jelly recipes are still seen. Edibility questionable as some people become ill after eating large quantities, not dangerous, see also page 135 ~~~ **Comments:** Swedish Dwarf Cornel, *Cornus suecica*, a similar species with leaves in pairs and flowers with maroon sepals grows in alpine areas. Hybridization occurs between the two species.

Capitate Valerian (Thoro Ridge)

Canadian Dogwood (Horseshoe Lake Trail)

Canadian Dogwood (Riley Creek)

Swedish Dwarf Cornel (Savage River)

Grove Sandwort (Mt. Healy)

Bering Sea Chickweed (Stony Creek)

TALL SANDWORT

Arenaria capillaris

(Pink / Caryophyllaceae)

Dry, rocky and sandy areas ~~~ Mid-June to early July ~~~ **Plant:** Perennial, clump ~~~ **Leaves:** Long, narrow (grass-like), usually light bluish-green ~~~ **Flowers:** Cup-shaped, about 5/8" on 3 to 4" stiff stems.

GROVE SANDWORT

Moehringia lateriflora

(Pink / Caryophyllaceae)

Woods ~~~ Late May to mid-June ~~~ **Plant:** Perennial, about 6" on horizontal rhizomes ~~~ **Leaves:** Opposite on stems, oval, pointed, thin, light green ~~~ **Flowers:** 5 rounded petals, about 3/8".

BERING SEA CHICKWEED

Cerastium beeringianum

(Pink / Caryophyllaceae)

Meadows or moist scree ~~~ Mid-June through July ~~~ **Plant:** Perennial, sprawling ~~~ **Leaves:** Opposite, oval, small ~~~ **Flowers:** 5 rounded indented petals, 5/8 to 3/4", cup-shaped ~~~ **Comments:** Field Chickweed or Mouse-ear Chickweed, *Cerastium arvense*, is a similar species having more pointed leaves and sterile side shoots (side branches with no flowers). Most we saw were in meadows and the plants were tall and reaching for light. In other localities they frequently grow on open stony slopes.

Tall Sandwort (Whitehorse, Yukon Territory)

TALL CAMPION

Silene repens

(Pink / Caryophyllaceae)

Rocky and grassy slopes ~~~ July to early August ~~~ **Plant:** Perennial, 8 to 12" ~~~**Leaves:** Narrow, hairy, opposite on flower stem ~~~ **Flowers:** 5 connected petals, white (occasionally pink), salverform, calyx of 5 connected pink to purplish sepals.

ALASKA STARWORT

Stellaria alaskana

(Pink / Caryophyllaceae)

Rocky slopes and scree ~~~ Mid-June to late July ~~~ **Plant:** 2 to 3" perennial on horizontal rootstock ~~~ **Leaves:** Bluish-green, smooth, opposite, stiff, broad, oval, pointed and clustered near the base ~~~**Flowers:** One per stem, 3/8 to 5/8", 5 petals split to look like 10, sepals at least as long as petals ~~~ **Comments:** 1) *S. monantha* is a similar plant, leaves not as close to base, sepals shorter than petals. 2) Long-stalked Starwort, *S. longipes*, leaves are bluish-green, narrow, more pointed, not compressed at base of stem, flowers slightly smaller, 3/8 to 1/2", 2 to 3 per stem, sepals shorter than petals. 3) *S. laeta* has slightly hairy green leaves and 3/8 to 1/2" flowers.

Tall Campion (Mt. Healy Overlook Trail)

Alaska Starwort (Mt. Healy)

Stellaria laeta (Highway Pass)

Long-stalked Starwort (Mt. Healy)

Arctic Sandwort (Mt. Galen)

Minuartia arctica (Thoro Ridge)

Northern Bedstraw (Park Entrance)

ARCTIC SANDWORT

Minuartia macrocarpa

(Pink / Caryophyllaceae)

Sandy and rocky areas in the mountains ~~~ June to early July ~~~ **Plant:** Perennial, loosely-matted ~~~ **Leaves:** Small, narrow, short, flat, 3 nerved (having 3 distinct parallel veins), hairs around edges ~~~ **Flowers:** One on each glandular stem, 5/8 to 3/4" cup-shaped, occasionally pinkish (var. rosea), sepals oblong, blunt, less than half as long as petals ~~~ **Fruit:** Seed capsules at least twice as long as sepals ~~~ **Comments:** 1) *M. arctica* is similar but leaves are nerveless, sepals are often purplish and about half as long as petals, plant is more loosely sprawling, leaves narrower, and seed capsules no more than twice as long as sepals. 2) *M. obtusiloba* is also similar with smaller leaves and smaller flowers, petals barely longer than sepals. There are also some sagina species in the Park. They are delicate plants close to the ground with small narrow leaves and flowers about 1/4" across. Most are white but pink might be encountered. 3) *Wilhelmsia physodes* is another low member of the pink family found along some rivers in the Park. Leaves are glabrous, seed pods round. See page 135.

NORTHERN BEDSTRAW

Galium boreale

(Madder / Rubiaceae)

Fields, open woodlands and low mountain slopes ~~~ July to mid-August ~~~ **Plant:** Perennial, up to 18", spreading by underground rhizomes ~~~ **Leaves:** Narrow, 4 in a whorl on square stems, 3-veined ~~~ **Flowers:** Very small, 4 petals ~~~ **Uses:** Seeds used as a coffee substitute, dried plants were once used as a mattress stuffing because square stems did not crush easily and some varieties have a pleasant aroma.

LARGE-FLOWERED WINTERGREEN

Pyrola grandiflora

(Wintergreen / Pyrolaceae)

Woods, thickets and meadows ~~~ Mid-June to late July ~~~ **Plant:** Perennial, 8 to 12" ~~~ **Leaves:** Basal, shiny, evergreen, thick, round, 1 to 2", frequently with pinkish stems ~~~ **Flowers:** Cup-shaped, 5/8 to 3/4", several, on a thick pinkish stem. ~~~ **Fruit:** Persistent, round, drooping, 5-parted seed capsule with protruding style.

SINGLE DELIGHT, SHY MAIDEN

Monesis uniflora

(Wintergreen / Pyrolaceae)

Woods, thickets, mostly at low elevations ~~~ Mid-June to mid-July ~~~ **Plant:** Perennial, 2 to 4" ~~~ **Leaves:** Evergreen, round, slightly pointed, thick, leathery, 1/2 to 5/8" on short stems ~~~ **Flowers:** 5 broad pointed waxy petals, facing downwards with a protruding style ~~~ **Fruit:** Persistent, round capsule with pronounced style, facing upwards.

Large-flowered Wintergreen (McKinley River Bar Trail)

Single Delight (Mt. Healy)

LAPLAND DIAPENSIA

Diapensia lapponica

(Diapensia / Diapensiaceae)

Gravelly spots in the tundra and rocky alpine ~~~ June to early July ~~~ **Subshrub:** Small, tight mats ~~~**Leaves:** Very small, hard, oval, evergreen in rosettes ~~~ **Flowers:** Flaring, cup-shaped on short stems, 5 joined petals ~~~ **Fruit:** 3-parted seed capsule.

Lapland Diapensia (Stony Dome)

Bell Heather (Mt. Healy)

BELL HEATHER

Cassiope tetragona

(Heath / Ericaceae)

Tundra and rocky alpine slopes (especially north-facing) ~~~ Mid-June to mid-July ~~~ **Shrub:** Matted evergreen, up to 8" ~~~ **Leaves:** Thick, hard, stacked tightly together in four rows on the stems (looking much like a Phillips screwdriver) ~~~ **Flowers:** Small, bell-shaped, aromatic.

Red Bearberry (Teklanika Campground)

RED BEARBERRY

Arctostaphylos rubra

(Heath / Ericaceae)

Bogs, tundra, below treeline ~~~ Late May to mid-June ~~~ **Shrub:** Dwarf ~~~ **Leaves:** oval, thin ~~~ **Flowers:** Creamy-white, very small, urn-shaped ~~~ **Fruit:** Red juicy berry beneath the leaves ~~~ **Uses:** Edible raw or cooked, a favorite of birds and bears ~~~ **Comments:** Alpine Bearberry, *Arctostaphylos alpina*, is a similar shrub, but with black berries, leaves are coarser and have hairs around margins, leaves turn scarlet in the fall. See also pages 122 & 138.

Alpine Bearberry (Polychrome)

Red Bearberry (Teklanika Campground)

LABRADOR TEA

Ledum palustre ssp. *groenlandicum*
(Heath / Ericaceae)

Bogs, woods up into alpine ~~~ Mid-June to mid-July ~~~ **Shrub:** Up to 2' ~~~ **Leaves:** 1 to 1-1/2" long, 1/8 to 1/3" wide, evergreen, hard, narrow, oval, with rolled under edges, dark green above, rusty beneath ~~~ **Flowers:** Small, white, open bells in cluster near ends of branches ~~~ **Fruit:** 5-parted seed capsule ~~~ **Comments:** Narrow Leaf Labrador Tea,*Ledum palustre* ssp. *decumbens*, is similar to above, but with very small, narrow leaves, usually found in bogs or alpine. Flowers may be pinkish.

Labrador Tea (Tetlin Jct.)

Narrow Leaf Labrador Tea (in seed)

HIGH-BUSH CRANBERRY

Viburnum edule
(Honeysuckle / Caprifoliaceae)

Woodlands and open low mountain slopes ~~~ June ~~~ **Shrub:** Up to 4 feet (taller in other locations) ~~~ **Leaves:** Variable, toothed, oval to rounded, with up to 3 to 5 lobes, turning red to maroon in the fall ~~~ **Flowers:** Very small, salverform, white to pinkish ~~~ **Fruit:** Red translucent berry with large flat seed, in clusters above the leaves (drooping when ripe) ~~~ **Uses:** Berries edible, sour, used in jellies, jam and syrups; also as a dye.

High-bush Cranberry (Anchorage)

High-bush Cranberry (Mt. Healy)

Narcissus-flowered Anemone (Savage River)

NARCISSUS-FLOWERED ANEMONE

Anemone narcissiflora

(Buttercup / Ranunculaceae)

Meadows and tundra ~~~ Early June to late July ~~~ **Plant:** Perennial up to 12", in clumps ~~~ **Leaves:** Basal on long stems, deeply divided, hairy ~~~ **Flowers:** 1 to 1-1/2", 1 or more on stem above a modified leaf that surrounds the stem, no petals, 5 to 10 oval sepals bluish on the back, stamens mostly in a tight cushion ~~~ **Fruit:** Flat seeds in a bunch, black when mature.

WINDFLOWER, NORTHERN ANEMONE

Anemone parviflora

(Buttercup / Ranunculaceae)

Meadows, along streams or in late snowbeds ~~~ Late May to early August ~~~ **Plant:** Perennial, 3 to 5", on horizontal rootstock ~~~ **Leaves:** Glabrous, basal, rounded in outline, divided into 3 sections and toothed, very dark early in the season ~~~ **Flowers:** 1 to 1-1/4", one per stem placed well above a modified leaf that surrounds the stem, flowers sway easily in the wind, no petals, 5 rounded sepals, white inside, bluish outside, cup-shaped, stamens loosely arranged when flower is mature ~~~ **Fruit:** Globular heads of small seeds attached to wooly carrier ~~~ **Comments:** 1) Blue Anemone, *A. drummondii*, has a smaller, more bluish flower with smaller, more deeply divided leaves. 2) *A. multiceps* is blue throughout and looks like a miniature Pasque Flower. See page 7.

Windflower (Mt. Margaret)

Windflower seed heads

Blue Anemone (Mt. Healy)

BEAR FLOWER, RICHARDSON'S SAXIFRAGE

Boykinia richardsonii

(Saxifrage / Saxifragaceae)

Meadows, near streams in the mountains ~~~ July and August ~~~ **Plant:** Perennial clump, up to 30" ~~~ **Leaves:** Large, round in outline, coarse-looking, toothed, on long stems, stem leaves reduced ~~~ **Flowers:** Long spike, 3/4 to 1", usually white with maroon sepals ~~~ **Uses:** A favorite of bears especially in young stage, also see page 47.

PRICKLY SAXIFRAGE

Saxifraga tricuspidata

(Saxifrage / Saxifragaceae)

Ridges and rocky outcroppings ~~~ June to early July ~~~ **Plant:** Perennial, 5 to 7", loosely matted, with many old dead leaves ~~~ **Leaves:** Wedge-shaped with 3 sharp teeth, evergreen, thick and leathery ~~~ **Flowers:** Many, on top of stem with a few small alternate leaves, 5 spotted creamy petals ~~~ **Fruit:** 2-pronged seed capsule.

TUFTED SAXIFRAGE

Saxifraga caespitosa

(Saxifrage / Saxifragaceae)

Rocky tundra ~~~ June ~~~ **Plant:** Tufted perennial, up to 4", with many old dead leaves ~~~ **Leaves:** In limp rosettes, 3 to 5 lobes narrowing at base ~~~ **Flowers:** Few, with 5 narrow, flaring petals on top of glandular-dotted stem having a couple of narrow alternate leaves.

Bear Flower (Quigley Ridge)

Tufted Saxifrage (Savage River)

Prickly Saxifrage (Mt. Healy)

Brook Saxifrage (Stony Dome)

BROOK SAXIFRAGE

Saxifraga punctata

[*Saxifraga nelsoniana*---Hultén 1973]

(Saxifrage / Saxifragaceae)

Wet meadows, near streams ~~~ Mid-June through July ~~~ **Plant:** Perennial, 6 to 10" ~~~ **Leaves:** In rosette, toothed, round to kidney-shaped, on long stems ~~~ **Flowers:** Small, 5-petaled, in loose raceme.

BULBLET SAXIFRAGE

Saxifraga cernua

(Saxifrage / Saxifragaceae)

Moist areas in the mountains ~~~ Late June and July ~~~ **Plant:** Perennial, 5 to 8" ~~~ **Leaves:** Small, round to kidney-shaped, with teeth, on long stems ~~~ **Flowers:** Solitary on top of long stem covered with new plantlets (vegetatively reproduced), note red bunches on stems.

ALPINE BROOK SAXIFRAGE

Saxifraga rivularis

(Saxifrage / Saxifragaceae)

Very wet areas, high alpine ~~~ July ~~~ **Plant:** Perennial, 2 to 3", in small clumps ~~~ **Leaves:** Very small, round to kidney-shaped, with teeth ~~~ **Flowers:** Very small, in loose clusters.

Bulblet Saxifrage (Primrose Ridge)

Alpine Brook Saxifrage (Sable Mt. Trail)

RED-STEMMED SAXIFRAGE

Saxifraga lyallii

(Saxifrage / Saxifragaceae)

Wet meadows and streams ~~~ July to early August ~~~ **Plant:** Perennial, up to 10" ~~~ **Leaves:** Basal, spatulate, broad at base, toothed at end, glabrous ~~~ **Flowers:** Small, 5 white petals, narrow at base, in a loose raceme at end of reddish stem ~~~ **Fruit:** 3 or 4 reddish, curved upright capsules.

REFLEXED SAXIFRAGE

Saxifraga reflexa

Saxifrage / Saxifragaceae)

Dry places in the mountains ~~~ June ~~~ **Plant:** Perennial, 5 to 7" ~~~ **Leaves:** Rosette, narrow base, toothed, broad, somewhat diamond-shaped, hairy on both sides ~~~ **Flowers:** 5 white petals nearly twice as long as sepals which are soon reflexed ~~~ **Fruit:** Purplish, ovate, pointed with fairly long style ~~~ **Comments:** Snow Saxifrage, *Saxifraga nivalis*, has leaves that are glabrous on top, petals are slightly longer than calyx.

SAXIFRAGA DAVURICA

Saxifraga davurica

[*Saxifraga calycina*---Hultén 1973]

(Saxifrage / Saxifragaceae)

Moist places in the mountains ~~~ July ~~~ **Plant:** Perennial, 4 to 6" ~~~ **Leaves:** Basal, glabrous, wedge-shaped (longer tapered base than Red-stemmed Saxifrage), with 5 to 7 pointed teeth ~~~ **Flowers:** 5 narrow petals, white to purplish, sepals purplish and slightly shorter than petals, reflexed in fruit ~~~ **Fruit:** Conical, purplish-black seed capsules with short style.

Red-stemmed Saxifrage (Stony Dome)

Reflexed Saxifrage (Wickersham Dome)

Saxifraga davurica (Thoro Ridge)

Grass of Parnassus (Morino Trail)

GRASS OF PARNASSUS

Parnassia palustris

(Saxifrage / Saxifragaceae)

Moist thickets, meadows, roadside ditches and river basins ～～ July and August ～～**Plant:** Perennial, up to 10" ～～ **Leaves:** Basal, light green, somewhat heart-shaped on short stems ～～**Flowers:** Up to 1", on long stems with one leaf, 5 pointed petals with obvious veins and a pronounced ovary ～～ **Fruit:** Conical seed capsule.

SMALL GRASS OF PARNASSUS

Parnassia kotzebuei

(Saxifrage / Saxifragaceae)

Alpine meadows and moist tundra ～～ July to early August ～～ **Plant:** Perennial, 2 to 6" ～～ **Leaves:** Somewhat heart-shaped, very small, in rosette ～～ **Flowers:** Very small, cup-shaped, on top of stem with 1 small leaf.

WHITISH GENTIAN

Gentiana algida

(Gentian / Gentianaceae)

Moist tundra and rocky slopes ～～ Mid-July to mid-August ～～ **Plant:** Perennial, up to 6" ～～ **Leaves:** Smooth, yellowish-green, opposite ～～ **Flowers:** Upright, tubular, flaring, creamy-white streaked with bluish-purple.

Small Grass of Parnassus (Stony Dome)   Whitish Gentian (Stony Dome)

KAMCHATKA ROCKCRESS

Arabis lyrata

(Mustard / Brassicaceae)

Open woods, dry rocky areas ~~~ Late May to early July ~~~ **Plant:** Perennial, 8 to 10", from tap root ~~~ **Leaves:** Basal rosette, lyre-shaped, alternate on stems ~~~ **Flowers:** 1/4", on branched stem ~~~**Uses:** Leaves edible raw or cooked, a favorite of animals.

LOW BRAYA

Braya humilis

(Mustard / Brassicaceae)

Dry scree slopes ~~~ June to mid-July ~~~ **Plant:** Perennial, 2 to 4", clump ~~~ **Leaves:** Mostly basal, alternate on stem, narrow, very hairy, occasionally with a few teeth ~~~ **Flowers:** Very small, in clumps at top of stems, sometimes purplish ~~~ **Fruit:** Long narrow seed capsule.

Kamchatka Rockcress (Savage River)

Low Braya (Mt. Healy)

Eschscholtz Draba (Stony Dome)

ESCHSCHOLTZ DRABA

Draba eschscholtzii

(Mustard / Brassicaceae)

Stream beds, meadows ~~~ July ~~~ **Plant:** Perennial, 2 to 4" ~~~ **Leaves:** Oval, pointed, flat, in small basal rosette which is somewhat flat to cup-shaped with a few branched hairs ~~~ **Flowers:** White or cream on slightly hairy leafless stem ~~~ **Fruit:** Capsule, glabrous, shorter than its stem ~~~ **Comments:** *Draba fladnizensis* has lanceolate leaves in rosettes with simple hairs and a few leaves on glabrous flower stems.

Draba hirta (Quigley Ridge)

DRABA HIRTA

Draba hirta

(Mustard / Brassicaceae)

Woods, thickets, rocky slopes ~~~ June ~~~ **Plant:** Perennial, 3 to 6" ~~~ **Leaves:** with simple, branched and stellate hairs, oval to wedge-shaped with coarse teeth, having basal rosette, alternate on flower stem ~~~ **Flowers:** Small and close together ~~~ **Fruit:** Glabrous seed capsule about as long as its stem ~~~ **Comments:** *Draba longipes* found in moist meadows is a similar taller plant, leaves are not toothed, and stem of seed capsule is longer than the capsule.

Snow Draba (Mt. Healy)

SNOW DRABA

Draba nivalis

(Mustard / Brassicaceae)

Dry rocky areas ~~~ Late May to late June ~~~ **Plant:** Perennial, 2 to 3", with long tap root ~~~ **Leaves:** Very small rosettes branching from base, covered with grayish hairs ~~~ **Flowers:** Very small, white, in cluster at end of leafless stem.

DRABA PSEUDOPILOSA

Draba pseudopilosa

(Mustard / Brassicaceae)

Rocky areas ~~~ June ~~~ **Plant:** Perennial with long branched tap root ~~~ **Leaves:** In dense rosettes, small, narrow lanceolate, hairy along edges, glabrous above, branched hairs below ~~~ **Flowers:** Small, on short leafless stem ~~~ **Fruit:** Oval, pointed, hairy seed capsule on a slightly shorter glabrous stem.

Draba pseudopilosa (East Fork River)
Photo-Marilyn Barker

Eutrema edwardsii, early stage (Mt. Galen)

EUTREMA EDWARDSII

Eutrema edwardsii

(Mustard / Brassicaceae)

Moist areas ~~~ June to early July ~~~ **Plant:** Slender perennial, up to 12" ~~~ **Leaves:** Basal, ovate, becoming narrower up the stem ~~~ **Flowers:** In terminal cluster elongating in age ~~~ **Fruit:** Long narrow upright seed capsule.

Alpine Bittercress (Savage River)

ALPINE BITTERCRESS

Cardamine bellidifolia

(Mustard / Brassicaceae)

Along alpine streams, moist rocky alpine slopes ~~~ July ~~~ **Plant:** Small perennial clump ~~~ **Leaves:** Clump, very small, oval, dark green, glabrous, pointed end with long stems ~~~ **Flowers:** Very small on short leafless stem ~~~ **Fruit:** Long narrow upright seed capsule ~~~ **Comments:** *Cardamine umbellata* has pinnately divided leaves on a 3 to 7" stem and is found in wet areas at low elevations.

Seed head

NORTHERN OXYTROPE

Oxytropis campestris

(Pea / Fabaceae)

Dry open fields, roadsides ~~~ June and July ~~~ **Plant:** Perennial clump, up to 14" ~~~ **Leaves:** Mostly upright, many, with many small pointed hairy leaflets ~~~ **Flowers:** Small, 10 to 15, usually white with purple tinge or yellow ~~~ **Fruit:** Erect, hairy, sessile pod.

Northern Oxytrope (Visitor Access Center)

Alaska Cotton Grass (Triple Lakes Trail)

ALASKA COTTON GRASS

Eriophorum brachyantherum

(Sedge / Cyperaceae)

Wet places ~~~ Late June to August ~~~ **Plant:** Perennial, small tufts ~~~ **Bristles:** Whitish ~~~ **Scales:** Dark ~~~ **Comments:** Other similar varieties are: 1) *E. scheuchzeri* which grows from runners and has large white heads. 2) *E. russeolum* with tannish to rust-colored bristles. 3) Tufted Cotton Grass, *E. vaginatum*, growing in dense clumps and having lead-colored scales, see page 134. 4) Tall Cotton Grass, *E. angusti-folium*, 8 to 20", with white bristles, 3 to 4 drooping heads, and leaves that are flat and broad.   5) *E. gracile* which is similar to the above but leaves are narrow and channeled (triangular in cross-section). 6) Small Cotton Grass, *Trichophorum alpinum*, is a smaller, clumping plant, up to 10", with many small wispy heads.

Small Cotton Grass (McKinley River Bar Trail)

Tall Cotton Grass (Savage River)

ROCK JASMINE

Androsace chamaejasme
(Primrose / Primulaceae)

Dry, rocky tundra and gravelly slopes ~~~
June to early July ~~~ **Plant:** Perennial,
2 to 3" ~~~**Leaves:** Hairy, very small,
in tight rosettes on trailing branches
~~~**Flowers:** About 1/3", white with
yellow eye, in clusters on a hairy leafless
stem.

NORTHERN JASMINE

Androsace septentrionalis
(Primrose / Primulaceae)

Dry slopes ~~~ Late May to early June ~~~
Plant: Up to 6", growing upright, reddish
in seed ~~~ **Leaves:** Flat rosette, slightly
hairy, slightly indented, turn red and wither
very early ~~~ **Flowers:** Many, very small,
white with yellow eye, in umbels ~~~ **Comments:** Alaska Jasmine, *Androsace
alaskana*, similar with many 2 to 3" stems
having 1 to 3 flowers each, upright in full
bloom and sprawling in seed.

Rock Jasmine (Savage River)

Alaska Jasmine (Thoro Ridge)
Photo-Forrest Baldwin

Northern Jasmine (Mt. Healy)

Alaska Jasmine (Knik Glacier)
Photo-Forrest Baldwin

Primula egalikensis (Moose Creek, Mt. Galen)

PRIMULA EGALIKENSIS

Primula egalikensis

(Primrose / Primulaceae)

Along streams or very wet meadows ~~~ Late June to mid-July ~~~ **Plant:** Slender perennial, up to 4" ~~~ **Leaves:** Few, basal, spatulate ~~~ **Flowers:** 2 or 3 at top of stem, 1/4" in size , occasionally lavender.

Star Flower

STAR FLOWER

Trientalis europea ssp. *arctica*

(Primrose / Primulaceae)

Woods, dry tundra ~~~ Mid-June to early July ~~~ **Plant:** Up to 5", perennial, on runners just below the surface ~~~ **Leaves:**Oval, slightly pointed, in a whorl around the stem, somewhat reddish early in the season ~~~ **Flowers:** Usually 7 pointed petals, sometimes pinkish ~~~ **Fruit:** Round silver-colored seed capsule.

Coral Root

CORAL ROOT ORCHID

Corallorrhiza trifida

(Orchid / Orchidaceae)

Moist woods or bogs ~~~ Late May to early June ~~~ **Plant:** Parasitic perennial with a root that looks like coral, 4 to 6" ~~~ **Leaves:** None ~~~ **Flowers:** Very small, near top of yellowish-green stem with a few narrow brownish sheaths, lower lip is white with purplish spots, calyx is 3 greenish-brown sepals ~~~ **Fruit:** Drooping seed pod.

COW PARSNIP

Heracleum lanatum

(Parsley / Apiaceae)

Woodlands and meadows ~~~ July ~~~ **Plant:** Perennial, up to 6 feet tall ~~~ **Leaves:** Very large, palmately lobed, toothed, hairy, on long stems attached to a thick, hairy stem ~~~ **Flowers:** Small, white, in slightly rounded double umbels ~~~ **Uses:** Raw stem (peeled) is edible ~~~ **Caution:** Irritating hairs on stems and leaves may cause an itchy rash and sun sensitivity resulting in blisters that may last for weeks.

Cow Parsnip (Wickersham Dome)

WILD CELERY

Angelica lucida

(Parsley / Apiaceae)

Thickets, moist meadows ~~~ July ~~~ **Plant:** Perennial, up to 24" ~~~ **Leaves:** 3-parted with coarse-toothed leaflets (somewhat like celery), inflated petioles (broadened where it joins to main stem) are somewhat translucent ~~~ **Flowers:** Very small in large double umbels, greenish-white ~~~ **Uses:** Edible like celery, coastal people inhaled fumes of boiled plant as a seasickness remedy.

Wild Celery (Thoro Ridge)

Cnidium cnidiifolium (Park Entrance)

CNIDIUM CNIDIIFOLIUM

Cnidium cnidiifolium

(Parsley / Apiaceae)

Dry, sunny areas near the Park entrance ~~~ July to mid-August ~~~ **Plant:** Perennial from long tap root, 20 to 30" ~~~ **Leaves:** Pinnately divided into 3 sections which are finely dissected ~~~ **Flowers:** Very small, white, in rounded double umbels.

Frigid Coltsfoot (McKinley Park Hotel)

FRIGID COLTSFOOT

Petasites frigidus

(Aster / Asteraceae)

Wet meadows and woodlands ~~~ Late May through June ~~~ **Plant:** Perennial, 10 to 18" ~~~ **Leaves:** Large, broadly triangular with wavy edges, sometimes shallowly lobed, from creeping root stock, whitish beneath, dark green and somewhat glossy above ~~~ **Flowers:** White to pinkish in heads clustered tightly together, usually flowering before the leaves on a short thick stalk extending at maturity, fluffing out like dandelion seed heads ~~~ **Comments:** Northern Coltsfoot, *Petasites hyperboreus*, is a similar species with deeply lobed leaves.

SIBERIAN YARROW

Achillea sibirica

(Aster / Asteraceae)

Fields and meadows ~~~ July and August ~~~ **Plant:** Perennial, 18 to 28", with many flower stalks ~~~ **Leaves:** Slightly hairy, long, narrow, with many sharp teeth ~~~ **Flowers:** Small, many, in flat-topped clusters ~~~ **Fruit:** Seeds in brown to tan, flat-topped clusters ~~~ **Comments:** Northern Yarrow, *Achillea borealis*, similar to above with finely dissected, pinnately divided leaves.

Northern Yarrow (Savage River)

Siberian Yarrow (Riley Creek)

CAT'S PAW

Antennaria monocephala ssp. *monocephala*

(Aster / Asteraceae)

Dry rocky areas in the tundra and alpine ~~~ Late June and July ~~~ **Plant:** Perennial, mat-like ~~~ **Leaves:** Spatulate in rosettes, hairy beneath, usually glabrous above ~~~ **Flowers:** Very small, in a dense head on a 2 to 3" stem with narrow leaves ~~~ **Comments:** *Antennaria monocephala* ssp. *philonipha* is similar but has stolons.

TALL PUSSY TOES

Antennaria pulcherrima

(Aster / Asteraceae)

Meadows ~~~ July ~~~ **Plant:** Perennial, up to 12" ~~~ **Leaves:** Long, narrow, hairy, grayish-green ~~~ **Flowers:** White, several heads in dense cluster.

PUSSY TOES

Antennaria friesiana

(Aster / Asteraceae)

Dry rocky areas in the tundra ~~~ Late June and July ~~~ **Plant:** Perennial, mat-like without stolons ~~~ **Leaves:** Long, lanceolate, densely hairy, grayish-green ~~~ **Flowers:** 2 to 5 heads in dense cluster, white to tannish on a 3 to 5" stem ~~~ **Comments:** *Antennaria isolepsis* is similar to above but has stolons and broader leaves, flowers mostly white, lower flower heads having longer stems than upper ones, making it a more flat-topped inflorescence.

Cat's Paw (Mt. Galen)

Pussy Toes (Mt. Healy)

Tall Pussy Toes (Highway Pass)

Erigeron lonchophyllus (Park Entrance)

ERIGERON LONCHOPHYLLUS

Erigeron lonchophyllus

(Aster / Asteraceae)

Moist places ~~~ July ~~~ **Plant:** Slender perennial, up to 10", with rough stems ~~~ **Leaves:** Long, narrow, hairs around edges ~~~ **Flowers:** Small, each head having a long stem ~~~ **Comments:** *Erigeron elatus* is similar to above but basal and stem leaves broader, flower stems shorter.

MOUNTAIN FLEABANE

Erigeron humilis

(Aster / Asteraceae)

Snow beds in the mountains ~~~ Late June through early August ~~~ **Plant:** Perennial, 2 to 3" ~~~ **Leaves:** Loose rosette, long-stemmed, spatulate, hairy, one or two per stem ~~~ **Flowers:** Single on hairy (often purplish) stem, one to a few, usually white becoming purplish, pappus white or tan ~~~ **Comments:** 1) *E. eriocephalus* is similar but more spreading, somewhat like a small mat, leaves mostly narrower, some on stems. Flowers usually white. Calyx, stems and leaves with many hairs. Grows in dry areas, pappus white or tan. 2) *E. purpuratus* with narrow leaves, flowers white turning purplish with age, calyx with purplish hairs.

Mountain Fleabane (Stony Dome)

Erigeron eriocephalus (Stony Creek)

Erigeron purpuratus (Thoro Ridge)

Miscellaneous Plants and Trees

Triple Lakes Trail
Late August, fall color of Shrub Birch, Alpine Bearberry and Balsam Poplar.

Moschatel (Mt. Healy)

MOSCHATEL, MUSKROOT

Adoxa moschatellina

(Moschatel / Adoxaceae)

Moist woodlands ~~~ Late May to early June ~~~ **Plant:** Perennial from whitish horizontal roots ~~~ **Leaves:** Yellowish-green with long stems, divided in 3-lobed leaflet (much like a Buttercup) ~~~ **Flowers:** 5, very small, in a tight cluster at the top of a 3 to 4" stem with 2 smaller leaves, the top flower has 4 sepals and 8 stamens; while the other 4 placed around the stem have 5 petals and 10 stamens.

ARENARIA CHAMISSONIS

Arenaria chamissonis

(Pink / Caryophyllaceae)

Alpine tundra and scree ~~~ Mid-June to mid-July ~~~ **Plant:** Perennial, low, loose cushion ~~~ **Leaves:** Very small and narrow ~~~ **Flowers:** Very small, green, (no petals), 5 green sepals, inconspicuous.

Arenaria chamissonis (Mt. Thorofare)

ROSEWORT, ROSEROOT

Sedum rosea

(Sedum / Crassulaceae)

Rocky slopes, meadows and ridges ~~~ June ~~~ **Plant:** Perennial ,up to 10" ~~~ **Leaves:** Stemless, alternate, thick, succulent, oval, pointed, with a few shallow teeth near the end (very variable) ~~~ **Flowers:** Very small, in dense cluster at top of stems, petals usually 4 and purplish (occasionally pink or yellow) ~~~ **Comments:** Dwarfed specimens 2 to 4" with bright green, strongly toothed leaves and red flowers can be found in rocky alpine areas of the Park. It is believed that these are cloned plants as they produce no seed.

Rosewort (Highway Pass)

Rosewort [dwarf form] (Mt. Healy)

SIDEBELLS PYROLA

Pyrola secunda

(Wintergreen / Pyrolaceae)

Woods, thickets ~~~ June to early July ~~~ **Plant:** Perennial, up to 5" ~~~ **Leaves:** Thick, glossy, evergreen, ovate, pointed and toothed ~~~ **Flowers:** 1/4" greenish bells along a curved stem ~~~ **Fruit:** Oval, green, with long protruding style, stem becoming slightly more upright at maturity.

Sidebells Pyrola (Mt. Healy)

TIMBERBERRY, NORTHERN COMANDRA, PUMPKIN BERRY

Geocaulon lividum

(Sandlewood / Santalaceae)

Woodlands ~~~ May to early June ~~~ **Plant:** Up to 6", probably semi-parisitic, on root runners ~~~ **Leaves:** Oval, pointed, often variegated, reddish in fall ~~~ **Flowers:** Small, green, close to main stem ~~~ **Fruit:** Round edible orange berry with very little flavor.

Timberberry (Horseshoe Lake Trail)

Timberberry (Anchorage)

Artemisia globularia (Mt. Healy)

ARTEMISIA GLOBULARIA

Artemisia globularia

(Aster / Asteraceae)

Rocky alpine slopes ~~~ June ~~~ **Plant:** Perennial, 2 to 4" ~~~ **Leaves:** Silvery, in a rosette, wedged at base, finely divided into narrow segments ~~~ **Flowers:** Dark maroon, in tight round head.

PRAIRIE SAGEWORT, FRIGID WORMWOOD

Artemisia frigida

(Aster / Asteraceae)

Dry sandy or rocky areas ~~~ Late June and July ~~~ **Plant:** Branched perennial, 8 to 12", from sturdy rootstock ~~~ **Leaves:** Silvery with fine hairs, finely dissected narrow segments, smells like sage ~~~ **Flowers:** Yellowish, small heads (like the center of a daisy) alternately on the stems ~~~ **Comments:** 1) Alaska Wormwood, *A. alaskana*, is a similar plant with slightly broader leaf segments. Although it is aromatic, it does not smell like sage. 2) *A. furcata* is very similar to Alaska Wormwood but has slightly broader leaf segments. Stems frequently reddish, silky when young, stem leaves are longer than flower heads. 3) Arctic Wormwood, *Artemisia arctica*, is a similar species without apparent odor and having green, shiny, non-hairy leaf segments. It is found in meadows and alpine tundra, see page 117.

Prairie Sagewort (Mt. Healy)

Arctic Wormwood (Mt. Healy)

Artemisia furcata (Mt. Healy)

PINK DANDELION

Taraxacum carneocoloratum

(Aster / Asteraceae)

Alpine scree and talus ~~~ Mid-June to early July ~~~ **Plant:** Perennial with long tap root ~~~ **Leaves:** 2 to 3" long, toothed ~~~ **Flowers:** Flesh-colored on drooping stem.

Pink Dandelion (Mt. Thorofare)

TALL WORMWOOD

Artemisia tilesii

(Aster / Asteraceae)

Woodlands ~~~ July ~~~ **Plant:** Perennial, 2 to 4 feet ~~~ **Leaves:** Dark green and shiny above, whitish and hairy beneath, aromatic, sharply dissected ~~~ **Flowers:** Yellowish-green, very small on branched stems ~~~ **Uses:** As a dried flower. A healing and soothing ointment is made from flower heads.

Tall Wormwood (Sanctuary River)

Alpine Meadow Rue (Quigley Ridge)

Alpine Meadow Rue (Mt. Galen)

ALPINE MEADOW RUE

Thalictrum alpinum

(Buttercup / Ranunculaceae)

Alpine meadows and rocky slopes ~~~ June and July ~~~ **Plant:** Perennial, up to 8" ~~~ **Leaves:** Mostly divided into 3's with small, round, toothed leaflets, glabrous, shiny and dark green above, dull and lighter green beneath ~~~ **Flowers:** Very small, mostly drooping, reddish-brown.

Stiff Stem Saxifrage (Mt. Galen)

STIFF STEM SAXIFRAGE, HAWK LEAF SAXIFRAGE

Saxifraga hieracifolia

(Saxifrage / Saxifragaceae)

Wet tundra and meadows ~~~ July ~~~ **Plant:** Perennial, up to 12", with stiff glandular stem ~~~ **Leaves:** In loose rosette, broad, lanceolate, tapering to base, slightly wavy edges, slightly reddish on underside ~~~ **Flowers:** 1/4 to 3/8", 5 green to purplish-brown, oblong to triangular petals, 5 triangular green sepals.

NORTHERN WATER CARPET

Chrysosplenium tetrandrum

(Saxifrage / Saxifragaceae)

Very wet meadows and edges of streams ~~~ Mid-June to early July ~~~ **Plant:** Perennial, 2 to 4", with slender root ~~~ **Leaves:** Small, green to greenish-yellow, glabrous, round to kidney-shaped, with shallow teeth, often clustered below the flowers, see below ~~~ **Flowers:** Cup-shaped, small green sepals, usually 4 stamens.

Northern Water Carpet (Mt. Healy)

CHRYSOSPLENIUM WRIGHTII

Chrysosplenium wrightii

(Saxifrage / Saxifragaceae)

Wet alpine scree slopes ~~~ July ~~~ **Plant:** Perennial, up to 2", with thick root ~~~ **Leaves:** Slightly hairy, round to kidney-shaped, with rounded teeth, mostly basal with some clustered below the flowers ~~~ **Flowers:** Very small, sepals green with purplish blotches.

Chrysosplenium wrightii (Mt. Healy)

RED BURNET

Sanguisorba officinalis

(Rose / Rosaceae)

Meadows ~~~ July ~~~ **Plant:** Perennial, up to 2 feet ~~~ **Leaves:** Coarse, pinnately divided with toothed oval leaflets. See Sitka Burnet, page 50 ~~~ **Flowers:** Very small, in tight spike, each with 5 maroon sepals and short stamens.

COMMON JUNIPER

Juniperus communis

(Cypress / Cupressaceae)

Dry rocky areas ~~~ **Shrub:** 1 to 3 feet, in large sprawling patches ~~~ **Leaves:** Evergreen, narrow (neddle-like), sharply pointed, bluish-green ~~~ **Fruit:** An oval cone, green at first becoming blue to black ~~~ **Uses:** Ground and used as a seasoning, distilled and used as flavoring in gin.

Red Burnet (Highway Pass)

CROWBERRY

Empetrum nigrum

(Crowberry / Empetraceae)

Woods and tundra ~~~ May to early June ~~~ **Shrub:** Low ~~~ **Leaves:** Evergreen, narrow, small, hard ~~~ **Flowers:** Small and inconspicuous, between leaves at ends of branches, maroon, no petals, 3 sepals, 3 stamens ~~~ **Fruit:** Round, black, shiny, seedy, sweet berry.

Common Juniper (Mt. Healy)

Crowberry (Mt. Healy)

Crowberry (Chugach Mts., Anchorage)

Gooseberry (Horseshoe Lake)

Red Currant (Triple Lakes Trail)

GOOSEBERRY

Ribes lacustre

(Gooseberry / Grossulariaceae)

Moist woods ~~~ June ~~~ **Shrub:** Up to 30", with thorns ~~~ **Leaves:** 1 to 1-1/2", 3 to 5-lobed, toothed (maple-like) ~~~ **Flowers:** 5 very small rosy-green sepals in racemes hanging under leaves ~~~ **Fruit:** Hairy, black, shiny, edible ~~~ **Uses:** Jellies, pies and syrups.

RED CURRANT

Ribes triste

(Gooseberry / Grossulariaceae)

Woods, occasionally sheltered alpine slopes ~~~ Late May to mid-June ~~~ **Shrub:** Up to 36", with shaggy bark ~~~ **Leaves:** To 3", toothed (maple-like), 3 to 5 lobed turning red in fall ~~~ **Flowers:** Very small, in loose racemes, hanging down beneath the leaves, 5 brick red sepals, petals very small and purplish ~~~ **Fruit:** Transparent red edible berries ~~~ **Uses:** Jelly and juice.

MOUNTAIN SORREL

Oxyria digyna

(Buckwheat / Polygonaceae)

Wet alpine meadows and rocky outcroppings along streams ~~~ July to early August ~~~ **Plant:** Perennial clump, 5 to 12" ~~~ **Leaves:** Long-stemmed, round to kidney-shaped, rather thick ~~~ **Flowers:** Very small, no petals, bracts usually reddish in dense branched spike ~~~ **Uses:** Leaves edible raw or cooked, sour-tasting (contain oxalic acid). A thirst quencher on the trail as it increases your saliva flow.

Mountain Sorrell (Thoro Ridge)

ARCTIC DOCK

Rumex arcticus

(Buckwheat / Polygonaceae)

Wet meadows ~~~ July ~~~ **Plant:** Perennial, 1 to 4 feet ~~~ **Leaves:** Thick, with a stem, lance-shaped with blunt end, stem leaves small and often pointed ~~~ **Flowers:** Small, no petals, in branched inflorescence on thick stalks, bracts reddish ~~~ **Uses:** Leaves cooked and eaten by Native Alaskans and early settlers.

Arctic Dock (McKinley River Bar Trail)

Sheep Sorrel (Mt. Galen)

SHEEP SORREL

Rumex acetosa ssp. *alpestris*

(Buckwheat / Polygonaceae)

Meadows in the mountains ~~~ July ~~~ **Plant:** Slender perennial, 12 to 30" ~~~ **Leaves:** Spade-shaped with long stems, stem leaves somewhat clasp the stem ~~~ **Flowers:** Small, no petals, bracts reddish, in slender branched inflorescences ~~~ **Uses:** Edible leaves.

Frog Orchid (Wickersham Dome)

FROG ORCHID

Coeloglossum viride ssp. *bracteatum*
(Orchid / Orchidaceae)

Meadows, moist woods ~~~ Mid-June to mid-July ~~~ **Plant:** Perennial, up to 15" ~~~ **Leaves:** Alternate on main stem, long spatulate with parallel veins ~~~ **Flowers:** Green, small, close together on a long spike, lower bracts between flowers at least twice as long as flowers ~~~ **Comments:** *Coeloglossum viride* ssp. *viride* is shorter with leaves close to base and lower bracts of flower spikes barely longer than flowers.

Northern Green Bog Orchid
(McKinley River Bar Trail)

NORTHERN GREEN BOG ORCHID

Platanthera hyperborea
(Orchid / Orchidaceae)

Bogs, wet ditches and meadows ~~~ Mid-June through July ~~~ **Plant:** Perennial, 6 to 14" ~~~ **Leaves:** Long, narrow, alternate on a thick stem, parallel veins ~~~ **Flowers:** Small, yellowish-green in a dense spike.

ONE-LEAF REIN ORCHID

Platanthera obtusata

(Orchid / Orchidaceae)

Moist mossy woods and bogs ~~~ Mid-June through July ~~~ **Plant:** Perennial, 5 to 7" ~~~ **Leaves:** Usually one from base of plant, broad, pointed at end, parallel veins ~~~ **Flowers:** Small, greenish, 3 to 6 at end of a slender stem.

One-leaf Rein Orchid (McKinley River Bar Trail)

Mare's Tail (Horseshoe Lake)

STRAWBERRY SPINACH, STRAWBERRY BLIGHT

Chenopodium capitatum

(Goosefoot / Chenopodiaceae)

Dry areas, roadsides ~~~ July to early August ~~~ **Plant:** 6 to 15", annual, often sprawling ~~~ **Leaves:** Long, spade-shaped, with slightly wavy edges ~~~ **Flowers:** Very small and inconspicuous ~~~ **Fruit:** Tight red bunches ~~~ **Uses:** Fruit used for jelly and syrup, leaves used like spinach.

MARE'S TAIL

Hippuris vulgaris

(Water Milfoil / Haloragaceae)

In shallow water ~~~ July ~~~ **Plant:** Perennial from creeping stem, partially submerged in water ~~~ **Leaves:** Glabrous, 6 to 12, narrow needle-like, in a whorl close together around stem ~~~ **Flowers:** Very small, inconspicuous below the water level.

Strawberry Spinach (Alaska Highway)

Fragrant Shield Fern (Mt. Healy)

FRAGRANT SHIELD FERN

Dryopteris fragrans

(Shield Fern / Aspidiaceae)

Rocky open slopes ~~~ **Plant:** 6 to 10" clump-type fern with many old dead stalks and curled old dead fronds persisting for at least one season ~~~ **Leaves:** Thick, stiff fronds with many rusty hairs ~~~ **Spores:** On underside of leaflets.

FRAGILE FERN

Cystopteris fragilis

(Lady Fern / Athyriaceae)

Rocky outcroppings and woods ~~~ Spreading by underground rhizomes ~~~ **Leaves:** Delicate fronds with thin glabrous leaflets ~~~ **Spores:** On underside of leaflets.

Fragile Fern (Wickersham Dome)

RUSTY WOODSIA

Woodsia ilvensis

(Lady Fern / Athyriaceae)

Dry rocky open areas ~~~ **Plant:** 4 to 6" clump-type fern with a few old dead stalks ~~~ **Leaves:** Coarse, pinnately divided fronds curled and silvery when young, rusty hairs on stems and underside, segments longer than broad ~~~ **Spores:** On underside of leaflets ~~~ **Comments:** 1) Smooth Woodsia, *W. glabella*, is 2 to 4" tall on horizontal rhizomes. Leaves are glabrous on both sides, segments about as broad as long. Spores on underside of leaflets. 2) Alpine Woodsia, *W. alpina*, is similar to *W. glabella*, but leaflets are hairy on underside.

Rusty Woodsia (Mt. Healy)

Smooth Woodsia (Quigley Ridge)

ALPINE LOVAGE

Ligusticum mutellinoides
[*Podistera macounii*---Hultén 1973]
(Parsley / Apiaceae)

Alpine meadows and moist rocky tundra ~~ Mid-June to early July ~~ **Plant:** Perennial, up to 3" ~~ **Leaves:** Basal, on long stems, glabrous, toothed, pinnately divided twice ~~ **Flowers:** Greenish-brown, in double umbels.

MOONWORT

Botrichium lunaria
(Adder's Tongue / Ophioglossaceae)

Grassy slopes and alpine meadows ~~ **Plant:** 2 to 4", soft thick stalk ~~ **Leaves:** One on stalk, thick, somewhat succulent, pinnately divided with roundish, overlapping leaflets with broad base and some wavy edges ~~ **Spores:** On fertile frond which is a continuation of leaf stalk ~~ **Comments:** Northern Moonwort, *Botrichium boreale,* is similar but has more deeply divided leaflets

Alpine Lovage (Mt. Galen)

Northern Moonwort (Mt. Healy)

Moonwort (Mt. Healy)

Common Club Moss (Mt. Healy)

COMMON CLUB MOSS

Lycopodium annotinum

(Club Moss / Lycopodiaceae)

Woods and rocky slopes ~~~ Spore bearing ~~~ **Plant:** Perennial, 3 to 5", on long creeping branches just below the surface of soil ~~~ **Leaves:** Small, stiff, narrow, yellowish-green, evergreen ~~~ **Comments:** 1) Creeping Jenny or Christmas Greens, *L. complanatum,* is a woodland species with small flat leaves in 4 rows on branched stems. Used as a rope and filler when making Christmas wreaths. It has somewhat the appearance of cedar. 2) Alpine Club Moss, *L. alpinum,* found on alpine tundra and scree in small branched clumps on horizontal stems. Color is variable but often bluish-green. 3) Fir Club Moss, *L. selago,* found on tundra in the mountains. This is a branched plant with small, round, flat, yellowish-brown (golden) leaves clustered near top of stems.

Creeping Jenny (Mt. Healy)

Fir Club Moss (Mt. Healy)

SMALL HORSETAIL

Equisetum variegatum ssp. *variegatum*

(Horsetail / Equisetaceae)

Woods, tundra and scree slopes ~~~ **Plant:** Perennial, 3 to 8", from horizontal stems ~~~ **Leaves:** None ~~~ **Branches:** Evergreen, green, rough, vertical branches with 6 to 8 flat-topped ridges ~~~ **Comments:** *Equisetum scirpoides* is a similar species in clumps with 6 to 8 v-shaped ridges, found in woods and tundra.

Small Horsetail (Sable Mt. Trail)

COMMON HORSETAIL

Equisetum arvense

(Horsetail / Equisetaceae)

Fields and woodlands ~~~ May~~~Spore-bearing phase occurs on a stalk lacking chlorophyll ~~~ **Plant:** Fast spreading 8 to 14" perennial from underground horizontal stems ~~~ **Leaves:** none ~~~ **Stems:** Very rough due to presence of silica, side branches green in whorls around the angled hollow stem, lower set of branches are very short ~~~ **Comments:** *Equisetum silvaticum* is a similar, more lacy-looking, species with forked branches, drooping at first. Spore capsule appearing on top of green stem ~~~ **Uses:** Works as a pot and pan scrubber due to silica content.

Equisetum scirpoides (Triple Lakes Trail)

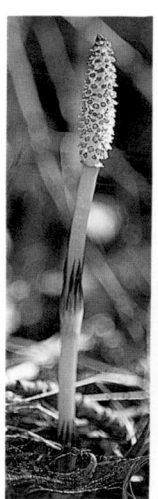 

Common Horsetail (Park Entrance)
Spore Phase   Vegetative Phase

Equisetum silvaticum (McKinley River Bar Trail)

Carex scirpoidea (Quigley Ridge)

CAREX SCIRPOIDEA

Carex scirpoidea

(Sedge / Cyperaceae)

Meadows and tundra ~~~ June ~~~ **Plant:** Loose clump ~~~ **Leaves:** Very long and narrow ~~~ **Flowers:** Showy heads of small flowers, one head per stem.

ALPINE HOLY GRASS

Hierochloe alpina

(Grass / Poaceae)

Alpine tundra ~~~ Mid-June to mid-July ~~~ **Plant:** 8 to 12" tall, usually taller than surrounding plants, small clump ~~~ **Leaves:** Long, narrow ~~~ **Flowers:** In somewhat triangular spikes, purplish at first, showy for size of plant.

ALPINE BLUE GRASS

Poa alpina

(Grass / Poaceae)

Alpine tundra ~~~ Late June to mid-August ~~~ **Plant:** Perennial, clump ~~~ **Leaves:** Short, narrow, flat, dry papery sheaths from previous years leaves ~~~ **Flowers:** In broad panicle ~~~ **Comments:** Seeds of the many grasses in the Park are food for birds and ground squirrels.

Alpine Holy Grass (Wickersham Dome)

Alpine Blue Grass

Arctic ground squirrel feasting on grass

MOUNTAIN ALDER

Alnus crispa

(Birch / Betulaceae)

Cleared and open areas, edges of woods up into the mountains ~~~ May to early June ~~~ **Shrub:** Branched, smooth gray branches with white blotches, 2 to 10 feet tall, forming dense thickets ~~~ **Leaves:** 2 to 4", oval, pointed, with shallow teeth, dark green and somewhat shiny above, lighter green below, turning black in fall, winter bud scales overlap ~~~ **Flowers:** Male--small in dense drooping catkins, female--upright above the catkins ~~~ **Fruit:** Seeds in a cone on long stems ~~~ **Comments:** *Alnus incana* is similar, leaves are dull, winter bud scales do not overlap, cones have short stems, mature shrub has a more reddish bark.

Mountain Alder (Riley Creek)

BROOMRAPE

Boschniakia rossica

(Broomrape / Orobanchaceae)

Lowlands to alpine ~~~ June ~~~ **Plant:** Parasitic plant on Mountain Alder (*Alnus crispa*) roots ~~~ **Leaves:** None, brown glabrous scales ~~~ **Flowers:** Betweeen scales, brownish-red to violet ~~~ **Comments:** Dried remains of previous years plants are visible early in the season. A yellow specimen was a rare find..

Mountain Alder (Drooping male catkins, and upright female catkins)

Broomrape (Wonder Lake)

Mt. Alder cones

Black Birch (Kantishna)

Paper Birch (Park Entrance)

BLACK BIRCH, KENAI BIRCH

Betula kenaica

(Birch / Betulaceae)

Woodlands mixed with spruce and cottonwoods ~~~ May ~~~ **Tree:** Up to 35 feet, reddish bark when young becoming gray to black in age, young twigs covered with resin dots ~~~ **Leaves:** 2 to 3", somewhat heart-shaped on long stems, finely toothed edges, turning yellow in fall ~~~ **Flowers:** Inconspicuous on a catkin ~~~ **Comments:** Paper Birch, *Betula papyrifera*, is a similar larger tree (up to 60 ft.),bark becomes white with age, hybridization occurs.

SHRUB BIRCH, RESIN BIRCH

Betula glandulosa

(Birch / Betulaceae)

Wet areas ~~~ May ~~~ **Shrub:** Up to 8 feet with resin dots on branches ~~~ **Leaves:** 5 / 8 to 1", oval, pointed, longer than broad, with fine teeth, turning orange or red in fall ~~~ **Comments:** Hybridization occurs with Paper Birch, the hybrid being known as Yukon Birch, *B. occidentalis*, This is a small tree or tall shrub, leaves are oval and pointed,butturn red in fall, see page 107. Dwarf Birch, *B. nana,* is similar to *B. glandulosa* but is shorter and has toothed, round leaves. See pages 112 & 128.

Shrub Birch (late August-Savage River)
See also pages 108 and 127.

WHITE SPRUCE

Picea glauca

(Pine / Pinaceae)

Woods, tundra and valleys up into the mountains ~~~ May to early June ~~~ **Tree:** 30 to 80 feet, with rough scaly bark, stems without hairs ~~ **Leaves:** Evergreen, 4-angled, bluish-green needles, 1/2 to 5/8" long with stomata on all sides ~~~ **Cones:** 1-1/2 to 2-1/2" long, developing in spring, falling off the following spring ~~~ **Comments:** Black Spruce, *Picea mariana*, is a smaller less shapely tree found growing in bogs, needles are dark green and shorter, twigs hairy and the egg-shaped cones remain on the tree for many years. Hybridization between the species is common, producing trees with mixed characteristics.

White Spruce (Mt. Healy)

Black Spruce (Just west of Park Headquarters)

Aspen & White Spruce forest

Balsam Poplar (Triple Lakes Trail)

Balsam Poplar (Kantishna)

BALSAM POPLAR, COTTONWOOD

Populus balsamifera

(Willow / Salicaceae)

River valleys following up stream beds ~~~ May to early June ~~~ **Tree:** Can be very large (up to 90 feet), with a very large trunk. Often stunted in the Park especially at high elevations. Bark very deeply grooved on mature trees, branches break easily ~~~ **Leaves:** Variable, 2 to 5", spade-shaped to oblanceolate, long-stemmed and long-pointed, shiny, turning yellow in fall ~~~ **Flowers:** Long catkins, male and female on separate trees.

QUAKING ASPEN

Populus tremuloides

(Willow / Salicaceae)

Open woods and sandy bluffs ~~~ May ~~~ **Tree:** Up to 36 feet, with smooth greenish bark, appearing nearly white on sunny side, bark on lower trunk somewhat grooved in age ~~~ **Leaves:** 2 to 2-1/2", broadly heart-shaped on long slender stems, trembling in a breeze, turning golden yellow in fall ~~~ **Flowers:** Catkins, male and female on separate trees ~~~ **Comments:** A pioneer tree that likes sunshine and dryness, see also page 111.

Quaking Aspen (Park Entrance)

ALASKA WILLOW, FELT LEAF WILLOW

Salix alaxensis

(Willow / Salicaceae)

Along rivers and creeks up into the mountains -- very abundant in the Park ~~~ May to early June ~~~ **Shrub or small tree:** Can be up to 30 feet, sometimes with a single trunk, new twigs white and wooly with dense felt-like hairs especially in winter and spring, bark gray and smooth, rough in age, sometimes forms "diamonds" ~~~ **Leaves:** 2 to 4", elliptical, a few hairs on top, densely hairy beneath (like felt), an obvious willow in creek beds as they look very silvery when a breeze blows the leaves ~~~ **Flowers:** On stout, sessile, very long upright catkins on the end of branches in spring, before leaves appear ~~~ **Comments:** Gray Leaf Willow, *S. glauca*, is a similar usually shrubby type willow (can be up to 20 ft.), leaves are oval to lanceolate with a dull gray look from hairs on both sides of leaves, catkins are on leafy twigs several inches back from end of branches, developing along with the leaves.

Alaska Willow (Tattler Creek)

BARRATT WILLOW

Salix barrattiana

(Willow / Salicaceae)

Low wetlands along rivers and streams into the mountains ~~~ Very abundant in the Park ~~~ Early June ~~~ **Shrub:** Very low, up to 2 feet, forming large loose clumps, twigs hairy ~~~ **Leaves:** Mostly standing upright, up to 2-1/2" long, grayish from long silky hairs, new buds very yellowish and apparent in mid-summer, new buds and leaves contain a yellow substance ~~~ **Flowers:** On large upright catkins at ends of branches, appearing before leaves. Male catkins very attractive, rose colored, see also page 111 ~~~ **Comments:** Barren Ground Willow, *S. niphoclada*, has a similar appearance, but leaves are much smaller, elliptical, yellowish-green (sometimes hairy on both sides). Catkins are set back from end of branches on short leafy twigs, appearing with the leaves. Can be up to 5 feet tall but usually dwarfed due to habitat, (dry rocky areas). See next page.

Gray Leaf Willow (Park Entrance)

Barratt Willow (Sanctuary River)

DIAMOND-LEAF WILLOW

Salix planifolia ssp. *pulcha*
(Willow / Salicaceae)

Bogs and wet thickets ~~~ June ~~~ **Shrub:** Up to 6 feet with old dead leaves present most of the time ~~~ **Leaves:** 1-1/2 to 2" long and 1/3 to 1/2" wide, diamond-shaped, green and shiny above, whitish beneath ~~~ **Flowers:** On catkins, on short leafless branches ~~~ **Comments:** Bebb Willow, *S. depressa* ssp. *rostrata*, has similar leaves slightly longer and whitish beneath, catkins are on short leafy twigs and each seed capsule is on a stem about 1/8" long (characteristic of this willow). It often develops diamond-shaped depressions on the trunks. These are caused by a fungus infection where a branch has broken off and are found on several willow species.

Diamond Leaf Willow (Savage River)

Diamond Leaf Willow (Teklanika River)

Barren Ground Willow (Bison Gulch)

Male Flowers

Female seed capsules

Diamond Willow

Bebb Willow (Park Entrance)

ARCTIC WILLOW

Salix arctica ssp. *arctica*
(Willow / Salicaceae)

Wet or dry tundra and alpine ridges ～～ June ～～ **Shrub:** Dwarf ～～ **Leaves:** Very hairy when young, oval to pointed (variable) ～～ **Flowers:** On very stout pinkish catkins on leafy stems ～～ **Fruit:** Hairy capsule ～～ **Comments:** 1) *S. arctica* ssp. *torulosa* has longer leaves with a wide rounded end and slightly narrower catkins on leafy stems, capsules are hairy at first and later glabrous, see also pages 108 & 128. 2) Netted Willow, *S. reticulata*, has more rounded leaves with obvious veins, leaves are dark green leathery and mostly glabrous, catkins are narrow and reddish on a leafless stem, capsules are hairy.

Arctic Willow-female catkins (Mt. Margaret)

Netted Willow (Mt. Galen)

Arctic Willow--male catkins

S. arctica ssp. *torulosa* (Polychrome Mt.)

Least Willow, female capsule (Mt. Healy)

Least Willow, male catkin (Quigley Ridge)

Skeleton Leaf Willow (Mt. Healy)

LEAST WILLOW

Salix rotundifolia

(Willow / Salicaceae)

Alpine tundra, frequently with lichens ~~~ Late May to early June ~~~ **Shrub:** Dwarf, mat-forming ~~~ **Leaves:** Very small, mostly round, leathery, some of previous years leaves remaining ~~~ **Flowers:** Pinkish, on very short few-flowered catkins ~~~ **Fruit:** Glabrous red seed capsules with obvious branched stigma ~~~ **Comments:** 1) Skeleton Leaf Willow, *S. phlebophylla*, is a similar alpine shrub but leaves are slightly longer and thinner. Remains of many old dead leaves are obvious, catkins are short, pinkish and hairy. 2) Setchell Willow, *S. setchelliana*, has thick, fleshy, spatulate, yellowish-green leaves on short branches that sprawl on the ground. It is found on gravelly river bars, capsules are on leafy stems and are large, glabrous and red.

Dwarf willow catkins in spring

Setchell Willow (Teklanika River)

MUSHROOMS

Mushrooms are spore-bearing fungi, growing from fine thread-like structures, feeding on decaying material. Some have limited habitats as they grow on specific matter. Many appear in late July and August with the increase of rain. Spore prints are needed for proper identification of most mushrooms, but a few are distinctive enough to be easily identified. Caribou, red squirrels, arctic ground squirrels and other small animals eat mushrooms. This is not a key to human edibility, however, as the digestive systems of animals and birds are different from those of humans.

Puff Ball (edible) inside looks like a marshmallow, solid and firm---no gills

Hedgehog Mushroom (*Hydnum imbricatum*) Edible, but bitter, might be confused with other inedible species. Has teeth under cap.

Bolete---edible in young stages, underside has spongy layer

Fly Agaric (*Amanita muscaria*)--**Poisonous**
Has gills and veil on stalk. Do not confuse young white button stage of this with puff balls.

LICHENS

Lichens abound in the Park due to nutrient poor soil. They are colonizers choosing specific habitats for each type and species. Most require careful studying and chemical tests to properly identify them. Therefore, we will touch very lightly on them in this publication. They are, however, an integral part of the Park flora as they are so common and some are the main source of food for caribou, especially in winter. Lichens have no chlorophyll so usually are not green, but different mineral type colors. They are composed of a fungus and alga living together (symbiotic relationship), each one benefiting from the arrangement. Dampness may cause some of them, especially the leafy lichens, to look green, due to presence of green or blue-green algae. Lichens reproduce by spores and vegetatively (sections of plants). Spores (Soredia) are sometimes produced on a podetia (stalk) which may be very short or cup-shaped. Soredia appear as a powdery substance, usually a different color than the lichen, often called the fruiting body. Lichens grow very slowly from a primary thalus (crust, plate or other structure). Some are attached by rhizines (coarse thread-like structures). Lichens have the ability of resting for long periods when conditions are not favorable, becoming very dry and and thus brittle.

Three growth types which might be encountered are:

Foliose Lichens---Leafy types --- those with somewhat loose lobes. Top and underside are different colors or texture. Grow in moist woods or on trees or rocks. Most have rhizines. Many foliose look like crustose but have free lobes.

Fruticose---Shrub-like or branched, growing on open ground, tundra or on trees. A favorite food of caribou. Attached directly to soil or trees--no rhizines.

Crustose---Like a crust on rocks or bark(frequently in alpine). Edges are tightly attached and will not lift off. No free lobes.

Old Man's Beard
(Hanging from
spruce trees)

Caribou feeding on willows in summer.

Hypogymnia sp. (on trees, woods)

Peltigera sp. (on ground, woods)

Cladonia bellidifolia (on ground, woods, and tundra)

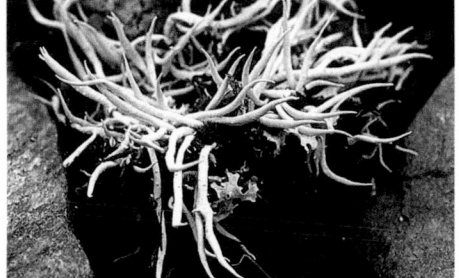

Thamnolia vermicularis (on ground, in alpine)

Crustose Lichen (on rocks in alpine)

Cetraria islandica
(on ground, open woods, tundra)

Cetraria sp. (on ground, alpine tundra)

Cladina stellaris & Steriocaulon sp.
(on ground, open tundra, dry woods)

Step Moss ---*Hylocomium splendens*

Ostrich Feather Moss---Ptilium crista-castrensis

Sphagnum Sp.

Stump with moss and lichen growth

MOSSES:

Mosses are spore-producing plants containing chlorophyll in their tiny leaves. They are attached to the soil by rhizoids (thread-like structures). They are colonizers, often growing in areas with poorly developed soil, or areas too wet for most flower-bearing plants. Many require careful scrutinizing to identify them, but a few can be recognized more easily and are common in the Park, mostly in bogs or moist woodlands in the east and west ends of the Park.

Feather Moss

Star Moss---*Polytrichum* sp.

Exploring Denali

There are many places to explore within and near Denali Park. The "General Management Plan" of the Park designates most areas beyond the Park Headquarters as "Wilderness" --- having no formal trails. It is, therefore, recommended that hikers disperse and find their own route rather than follow existing trails or create new ones. Most existing trails probably originated as game trails. Experience in other parks with heavy usage has shown that concentrated use of a single trail can cause deep, ugly ruts and/or tundra destruction and a "non-wilderness" appearance. Wherever you go, try to leave no evidence behind that you have been there. The Visitor Access Center is available for assistance, maps and a bookstore. We found the following publications to be very helpful: "The Nature of Denali"---by Sheri Forbes (Alaska Natural History Association)---a very good trail guide to the Park entrance area. "Exploring Mt. McKinley National Park"---by Richard W. Montague (Alaska Travel Publications)---although some information is outdated, it has a lot of valuable road and trail information. "The Denali Road Guide"---by Kim Heacox (Alaska Natural History Association)---a very nice, mile by mile, account of what to expect. "15 Hikes in Denali National Park"---by Don Croner (Transalaska Publ. Co.)---an excellent trail guide with maps.

Polychrome Mt. Back Country
Scamman's Spring Beauty, Macoun's Poppy

"Torn-up Tundra"
Damage done by grizzlies digging out Bear Flowers

Entrance area

Included in this list are plants that we saw while walking the trails to Horseshoe Lake, Triple Lakes, Morino Loop and along roadsides and in campground areas. Most of this is easy hiking on good trails; however, Triple Lakes Trail has some very wet and boggy areas. (Note: Horseshoe Lake Trail and Triple Lakes Trail were originally established in 1939). Wet and dry woods, roadsides, bogs and streams were encountered in making the list for this area. Much of it is good red squirrel and moose habitat.

Horseshoe Lake from Horseshoe Lake Trail

Spruce burls
(Horseshoe Lake)

_____	*Achillea borealis*	Northern Yarrow
_____	*Achillea sibirica*	Siberian Yarrow
_____	*Aconitum delphinifolium*	Monkshood
_____	*Alnus crispa*	Mountain Alder
_____	*Androsace chamaejasme*	Rock Jasmine
_____	*Anemone narcissiflora*	Narcissus-flowered Anemone
_____	*Anemone parviflora*	Windflower
_____	*Arabis lyrata*	Kamchatka Rockcress
_____	*Arctostaphylos rubra*	Red Bearberry
_____	*Arctostaphylos uva-ursi*	Kinnnikinnick
_____	*Arnica alpina* ssp. *attenuata*	Tall Alpine Arnica
_____	*Arnica frigida*	Frigid Arnica
_____	*Artemisia tilesii*	Tall Wormwood
_____	*Aster sibiricus*	Siberian Aster
_____	*Astragalus alpinus*	Alpine Mild Vetch
_____	*Betula glandulosa*	Shrub Birch
_____	*Betula nana*	Dwarf Birch
_____	*Betula occidentalis*	Yukon Birch
_____	*Betula papyrifera*	Paper Birch
_____	*Boschniakia rossica*	Broom Rape
_____	*Castilleja elegans*	Elegant Paintbrush
_____	*Chenopodium capitatum*	Strawberry Spinach
_____	*Cornus canadensis*	Canadian Dwarf Dogwood
_____	*Corydalis sempervirens*	Pale Corydalis
_____	*Delphinium glaucum*	Larkspur
_____	*Empetrum nigrum*	Crowberry
_____	*Epilobium angustifolium*	Common Fireweed
_____	*Epilobium latifolium*	Dwarf Fireweed
_____	*Equisetum arvense*	Field Horsetail
_____	*Equisetum pratense*	
_____	*Equisetum scirpoides*	
_____	*Equisetum variegatum* ssp. *variegatum*	Horsetail
_____	*Erigeron acris*	Blue Fleabane
_____	*Erigeron elatus*	
_____	*Erigeron lonchophyllus*	Long Leaf Fleabane
_____	*Eriophorum scheuchzeri*	Cotton Grass
_____	*Gentiana propingua*	Four-parted Gentian
_____	*Geocaulon lividum*	Timberberry
_____	*Hedysarum alpinum*	Eskimo Potato
_____	*Hedysarum mackenzii*	Wild Sweet Pea
_____	*Hordeum jubatum*	Squirrel-tail Grass
_____	*Juniperus communis*	Common Juniper
_____	*Ledum decumbens*	Narrow-leaf Labrador Tea
_____	*Ledum palustre*	Labrador Tea
_____	*Lepidium* sp.	Peppergrass

_____	*Linnaea borealis*	Twinflower
_____	*Lupinus arcticus*	Arctic Lupine
_____	*Luzula arctica*	Arctic Wood Rush
_____	*Lycopodium annotinum*	Stiff Club Moss
_____	*Matricaria matricarioides*	Pineapple Weed
_____	*Mertensia paniculata*	Bluebells
_____	*Moehringia lateriflora*	Grove Sandwort
_____	*Monesis uniflora*	Single Delight
_____	*Myosotis alpestris* ssp. *asiatica*	Alpine Forget-Me-Not
_____	*Oxytropis campestris*	Field Oxytrope
_____	*Papaver macounii*	Macoun's Poppy
_____	*Parnassia palustris*	Grass of Parnassus
_____	*Pedicularis labradorica*	Labrador Lousewort
_____	*Pedicularis verticillata*	Whorled-leaf Lousewort
_____	*Petasites frigidus*	Frigid Coltsfoot
_____	*Picea glauca*	White Spruce
_____	*Plantago major*	Common Plantain
_____	*Platanthera hyperborea*	Northern Green Bog Orchid
_____	*Platanthera obtusata*	One-leaf Rein Orchid
_____	*Polemonium acutiflorum*	Tall Jacob's Ladder
_____	*Polygonum alaskanum*	Wild Rhubarb
_____	*Populus balsamifera*	Cottonwood
_____	*Populus tremuloides*	Quaking Aspen
_____	*Potentilla fruticosa*	Tundra Rose
_____	*Potentilla multifida*	
_____	*Potentilla norvegica* ssp. *monspeliens*	Norwegian Cinquefoil
_____	*Pulsatilla patens* ssp. *multifida*	Pasqueflower
_____	*Pyrola asarifolia*	Pink Pyrola
_____	*Pyrola grandiflora*	Lg. Flowered Pyrola
_____	*Pyrola secunda*	Sidebells Pyrola
_____	*Rosa acicularis*	Prickly Rose
_____	*Rubus arcticus*	Nagoonberry
_____	*Rubus chamaemorus*	Cloudberry
_____	*Rubus idaeus*	Raspberry
_____	*Salix alaxensis*	Alaska Willow
_____	*Salix arbusculoides*	Little Tree Willow
_____	*Salix arctica* ssp. *crassijulis*	Arctic Willow
_____	*Salix depressa*	Bebb Willow
_____	*Salix fuscescens*	Alaska Bog Willow
_____	*Salix glauca*	Grayleaf Willow
_____	*Salix monticola*	Park Willow
_____	*Salix niphoclada*	Barren Ground Willow
_____	*Salix reticulata*	Net-leaf Willow
_____	*Salix scouleriana*	Scouler's Willow

_____ *Saussurea angustifolia* ....
_____ *Saxifraga tricuspidata* .... Prickly Saxifrage
_____ *Senecio lugens* .... Black-tipped Groundsel
_____ *Senecio pauciflorus* .... Few-flowered Senecio
_____ *Shepherdia canadensis* .... Soapberry
_____ *Solidago multiradiata* .... Northern Goldenrod
_____ *Taraxacum* sp. .... Common Dandelion
_____ *Vaccinium uliginosum* .... Bog Blueberry
_____ *Vaccinium vitis-idaea* .... Low-bush Cranberry
_____ *Viburnum edule* .... High-bush Cranberry
_____ *Viola epipsila* .... Marsh Violet
_____ *Zygadenus elegans* .... Death Camas

Red Squirrel (Park Entrance)

Yukon Birch (Triple Lakes Trail)

Alaska Wormwood (Mt. Healy)

Bus Travel

Included in this list are plants easily seen from a bus from the Visitor Access Center to Eielson Visitor Center. Mostly roadside, woods, thickets and tundra observed. All kinds of wildlife are visible.

Highway Pass
Fall color---Shrub Birch (red), Dwarf Willows (yellow)

Frigid Arnica

Grizzly eating grass

_____	*Achillea borealis*	Northern Yarrow
_____	*Achillea sibirica*	Siberian Yarrow
_____	*Aconitum delphinifolium*	Monkshood
_____	*Alnus crispa*	Mountain Alder
_____	*Anemone narcissiflora*	Narcissus-flowered Anemone
_____	*Anemone parviflora*	Windflower
_____	*Anemone richardsonii*	Yellow Anemone
_____	*Angelica lucida*	Wild Celery
_____	*Antennaria friesiana*	White Pussy-toes
_____	*Arctostaphylos alpina*	Alpine Bearberry
_____	*Arctostaphylos uva-ursi*	Kinnnikinnick
_____	*Arnica Alpina* ssp. *attenuata*	Tall Alpine Arnica
_____	*Arnica frigida*	Frigid Arnica
_____	*Arnica lessingii*	Lessing's Arnica
_____	*Artemisia arctica*	Arctic Wormwood
_____	*Artemisia frigida*	Prairie Sagewort
_____	*Artemisia tilesii*	Tall Wormwood
_____	*Aster sibiricus*	Siberian Aster
_____	*Astragalus alpinus*	Alpine Mild Vetch
_____	*Astragalus umbellatus*	Hairy Arctic Milk Vetch
_____	*Betula glandulosa*	Shrub Birch
_____	*Betula nana*	Dwarf Birch
_____	*Betula papyrifera*	Paper Birch
_____	*Boykinia richardsonii*	Alaska Boykinia
_____	*Campanula lasiocarpa* ssp. *lasiocarpa*	Mt. Harebell
_____	*Cardamine purpurea*	Purple Cress
_____	*Castilleja elegans*	Elegant Paintbrush
_____	*Claytonia scammaniana*	Scammen's Spring Beauty
_____	*Cornus canadensis*	Canadian Dwarf Dogwood
_____	*Delphinium glaucum*	Larkspur
_____	*Diapensia lapponica*	Lapland Diapensia
_____	*Dodecatheon frigidum*	Frigid Shooting Star
_____	*Draba hirta*	
_____	*Draba longipes*	
_____	*Dryas integrifolia*	Entire-leaf Avens
_____	*Dryas octopetala*	Mountain Avens
_____	*Empetrum nigrum*	Crowberry
_____	*Epilobium angustifolium*	Common Fireweed
_____	*Epilobium latifolium*	Dwarf Fireweed
_____	*Equisetum arvense*	Field Horsetail
_____	*Equisetum silvaticum*	Woodland Horsetail
_____	*Eriophorum angustifolium*	Tall Cotton Grass
_____	*Eriophorum scheuchzeri*	Cotton Grass
_____	*Galium boreale*	Northern Bedstraw
_____	*Geocaulon lividum*	Timberberry

_____	*Geranium erianthum*	Wild Geranium
_____	*Geum rossii*	Ross Avens
_____	*Hedysarum alpinum*	Eskimo Potato
_____	*Heracleum lanatum*	Cow Parsnip
_____	*Hordeum jubatum*	Squirrel-tail Grass
_____	*Ledum palustre*	Labrador Tea
_____	*Lupinus arcticus*	Arctic Lupine
_____	*Mertensia paniculata*	Bluebells
_____	*Myosotis alpestris* ssp. *asiatica*	Alpine Forget-Me-Not
_____	*Oxytropis campestris*	Field Oxytrope
_____	*Oxytropis nigrescens*	Purple Oxytrope
_____	*Oxytropis viscida*	Sticky Oxytrope
_____	*Papaver lapponicum*	Lapland Poppy
_____	*Parnassia palustris*	Grass of Parnassus
_____	*Parrya nudicaulis* ssp. *interior*	Parry's Wallflower
_____	*Pedicularis capitata*	Capitate Lousewort
_____	*Pedicularis kanei*	Wooly Lousewort
_____	*Petasites frigidus*	Frigid Coltsfoot
_____	*Picea glauca*	White Spruce
_____	*Picea mariana*	Black Spruce
_____	*Polemonium acutiflorum*	Tall Jacob's Ladder
_____	*Polygonum alaskanum*	Wild Rhubarb
_____	*Polygonum bistorta* ssp. *plumosum*	Pink Plumes
_____	*Populus balsamifera*	Cottonwood
_____	*Populus tremuloides*	Quaking Aspen
_____	*Potentilla biflora*	Two-flowered Cinquefoil
_____	*Potentilla fruticosa*	Tundra Rose
_____	*Potentilla uniflora*	One-flowered Cinquefoil
_____	*Pulsatilla patens* ssp. *multifida*	Pasqueflower
_____	*Pyrola asarifolia*	Pink Pyrola
_____	*Pyrola grandiflora*	Lg. Flowered Pyrola
_____	*Rhododendron lapponicum*	Lapland Rhododendron
_____	*Rosa acicularis*	Prickly Rose
_____	*Rubus arcticus*	Nagoonberry
_____	*Rumex arcticus*	Arctic Dock
_____	*Salix alaxensis*	Alaska Willow
_____	*Salix arctica* ssp. *crassijulis*	Arctic Willow
_____	*Salix arctica* ssp. *tortulosa*	Arctic Willow
_____	*Salix depressa*	Bebb Willow
_____	*Salix glauca*	Grayleaf Willow
_____	*Salix monticola*	Park Willow
_____	*Salix myrtillifolia*	Low Blueberry Willow
_____	*Salix pulcha*	Diamond Leaf Willow
_____	*Salix reticulata*	Net-leaf Willow
_____	*Sanguisorba stipulata*	Sitka Burnet

_____ *Saussurea angustifolia* ....

_____ *Saxifraga oppositifolia* .... Purple Mt. Saxifrage

_____ *Saxifraga tricuspidata* .... Prickly Saxifrage

_____ *Senecio atropurpureus* ....

_____ *Senecio fuscatus* ....

_____ *Senecio lugens* .... Black-tipped Groundsel

_____ *Shepherdia canadensis* .... Soapberry

_____ *Silene acaulis* ssp. *acaulis* .... Moss Campion

_____ *Solidago multiradiata* .... Northern Goldenrod

_____ *Spiraea beauverdiana* .... Alaska Spiraea

_____ *Vaccinium uliginosum* .... Bog Blueberry

_____ *Vaccinium vitis-idaea* .... Low-bush Cranberry

_____ *Valeriana capitata* .... Capitate Valerian

_____ *Viburnum edule* .... High-bush Cranberry

_____ *Zygadenus elegans* .... Death Camas

Aspen
colonizing slope (Igloo Creek)

Alpine Meadow Bistort
new plantlets

Mt. Healy

Easy access to Mt. Healy makes it a popular hiking area. Included in this list are plants we saw along the Mt. Healy Overlook Trail (starting from the Park Hotel) and from access points outside the Park. The vegetation is very variable from these different access points, but involves a lot of strenuous hiking. Woods, bogs, tundra, scree and talus habitats are included. Lower elevations on the Mt. Healy Overlook Trail are good moose habitat.

Mt. Healy as seen from the Park Road

Moose (Mt. Healy Overlook Trail)

Dwarf Birch

_____	*Achillea borealis*	Northern Yarrow
_____	*Aconitum delphinifolium*	Monkshood
_____	*Adoxa moschatellina*	Muskroot
_____	*Alnus crispa*	Mountain Alder
_____	*Androsace chamaejasme*	Rock Jasmine
_____	*Androsace septentrionalis*	Northern Jasmine
_____	*Anemone drummondii*	Blue Anemone
_____	*Anemone narcissiflora*	Narcissus-flowered Anemone
_____	*Anemone parviflora*	Windflower
_____	*Anemone richardsonii*	Yellow Anemone
_____	*Antennaria friesiana*	White Pussy-toes
_____	*Antennaria monocephala*	Cat's Paw
_____	*Antennaria pallida*	
_____	*Arabis lyrata*	Kamchatka Rockcress
_____	*Arctostaphylos alpina*	Alpine Bearberry
_____	*Arctostaphylos rubra*	Red Bearberry
_____	*Arctostaphylos uva-ursi*	Kinnikinnick
_____	*Arenaria capillaris*	Tall Sandwort
_____	*Arenaria chamissonis*	
_____	*Arnica alpina*	Alpine Arnica
_____	*Arnica frigida*	Frigid Arnica
_____	*Arnica lessingii*	Lessing's Arnica
_____	*Artemisia arctica*	Arctic Wormwood
_____	*Artemisia frigida*	Prairie Sagewort
_____	*Artemisia furcata*	
_____	*Artemisia globularia*	
_____	*Artemisia tilesii*	Tall Wormwood
_____	*Aster sibiricus*	Siberian Aster
_____	*Astragalus alpinus*	Alpine Milk Vetch
_____	*Betula glandulosa*	Shrub Birch
_____	*Betula nana*	Dwarf Birch
_____	*Betula occidentalis*	Yukon Birch
_____	*Betula papyrifera*	Paper Birch
_____	*Boschniakia rossica*	Broom Rape
_____	*Botrychium boreale*	Northern moonwort
_____	*Botrychium lunaria*	Moonwort
_____	*Boykinia richardsonii*	Alaska Boykinia
_____	*Bupleurum triradiatum*	Thoroughwort
_____	*Campanula lasiocarpa* ssp. *lasiocarpa*	Mt. Harebell
_____	*Campanula uniflora*	One-flowered Harebell
_____	*Cardamine bellidifolia*	Alpine Bittercress
_____	*Cardamine purpurea*	Purple Cress
_____	*Cassiope tetragona*	Bell Heather
_____	*Castilleja caudata*	

_____	*Castilleja elegans*	Elegant Paintbrush
_____	*Cerastrium beeringianum*	Bering Sea Chickweed
_____	*Chrysanthemum arcticum* ssp. *polare*	Arctic Chrysanthemum
_____	*Chrysosplenium tetrandrum*	Northern Water Carpet
_____	*Chrysosplenium wrightii*	
_____	*Cornus canadensis*	Canadian Dwarf Dogwood
_____	*Cornus suecica*	Lapland Dogwood
_____	*Cystopteris montana*	
_____	*Diapensia lapponica*	Lapland Diapensia
_____	*Douglasia gormanii*	Douglasia
_____	*Draba aurea*	
_____	*Draba cineraria*	
_____	*Draba hirta*	
_____	*Draba nivalis*	Snow Draba
_____	*Draba stenopetala*	
_____	*Dryas integrifolia*	Entire-leaf Avens
_____	*Dryas octopetala*	Mountain Avens
_____	*Dryopteris fragrans*	Fragrant Shield Fern
_____	*Empetrum nigrum*	Crowberry
_____	*Epilobium angustifolium*	Common Fireweed
_____	*Epilobium latifolium*	Dwarf Fireweed
_____	*Equisetum arvense*	Field Horsetail
_____	*Equisetum palustre*	Marsh Horsetail
_____	*Equisetum scirpoides*	
_____	*Equisetum variegatum* ssp. *variegatum*	Horsetail
_____	*Erigeron elatus*	
_____	*Erigeron eriocephalus*	
_____	*Erigeron hyperboreus*	
_____	*Eriophorum angustifolium*	Tall Cotton Grass
_____	*Eritrichium aretioides*	Mt. Forget-Me-Not
_____	Eritrichium splendens	Splendid Forget-Me-Not
_____	*Galium boreale*	Northern Bedstraw
_____	*Gentiana propingua*	Four-parted Gentian
_____	*Gentiana prostrata*	Moss Gentian
_____	*Geocaulon lividum*	Timberberry
_____	*Geum macrophyllum*	Large-leaf Avens
_____	*Geum rossii*	Ross Avens
_____	*Hedysarum alpinum*	Eskimo Potato
_____	*Hedysarum hedysaroides*	
_____	*Juniperus communis*	Common Juniper
_____	*Ledum decumbens*	Narrow-leaf Labrador Tea
_____	*Ledum palustre*	Labrador Tea
_____	*Ligusticum mutellinoides*	Alpine Lovage
_____	*Linnaea borealis*	Twinflower

_____	*Lloydia serotina*	Alp Lily
_____	*Loiseleuria procumbens*	Alpine Azalea
_____	*Lupinus arcticus*	Arctic Lupine
_____	*Luzula parviflora*	Few-flowered Wood Rush
_____	*Lycopodium annotinum*	Stiff Club Moss
_____	*Lycopodium complanatum*	Creeping Jenny
_____	*Lycopodium selago*	Fir Club Moss
_____	*Melandrium apetalum*	
_____	*Mertensia paniculata*	Bluebells
_____	*Minuartia arctica*	Arctic Sandwort
_____	*Minuartia rubella*	
_____	*Moehringia lateriflora*	Grove Sandwort
_____	*Oxyria digyna*	Mountain Sorrel
_____	*Oxytropis campestris*	Field Oxytrope
_____	*Oxytropis deflexa* ssp. *foliolosa*	
_____	*Oxytropis nigresens*	Purple Oxytrope
_____	*Oxytropis viscida*	Sticky Oxytrope
_____	*Papaver alaskanum*	Alaska Poppy
_____	*Parnassia kotzebuei*	Small Grass of Parnassus
_____	*Parnassia palustris*	Grass of Parnassus
_____	*Pedicularis capitata*	Capitate Lousewort
_____	*Pedicularis kanei*	Wooly Lousewort
_____	*Pedicularis labradorica*	Labrador Lousewort
_____	*Pedicularis oederi*	Oederi's Lousewort
_____	*Pedicularis verticillata*	Whorled-leaf Lousewort
_____	*Petasites frigidus*	Frigid Coltsfoot
_____	*Picea glauca*	White Spruce
_____	*Poa alpina*	Alpine Blue Grass
_____	*Poa arctica*	Arctic Blue Grass
_____	*Polemonium acutiflorum*	Tall Jacob's Ladder
_____	*Polygonum alaskanum*	Wild Rhubarb
_____	*Polygonum viviparum*	Alpine Meadow Bistort
_____	*Populus balsamifera*	Cottonwood
_____	*Populus tremuloides*	Quaking Aspen
_____	*Potentilla biflora*	Two-flowered Cinquefoil
_____	*Potentilla fruticosa*	Tundra Rose
_____	*Potentilla hookeriana*	Hooker's Cinquefoil
_____	*Potentilla hyparctica*	
_____	*Potentilla norvegica* ssp. *monspeliens*	Norwegian Cinquefoil
_____	*Potentilla uniflora*	One-flowered Cinquefoil
_____	*Primula egaliksensis*	Greenland Primrose
_____	*Pulsatilla patens* ssp. *multifida*	Pasqueflower
_____	*Pyrola asarifolia*	Pink Pyrola
_____	*Pyrola grandiflora*	Lg. Flowered Pyrola

_____	*Pyrola minor*	Small Flowered Pyrola
_____	*Pyrola secunda*	Sidebells Pyrola
_____	*Ranunculus nivalis*	Snow Buttercup
_____	*Rhododendron lapponicum*	Lapland Rhododendron
_____	*Ribes triste*	Red Currant
_____	*Rosa acicularis*	Prickly Rose
_____	*Rubus arcticus*	Nagoonberry
_____	*Rubus chamaemorus*	Cloudberry
_____	*Rubus idaeus*	Raspberry
_____	*Salix alaxensis*	Alaska Willow
_____	*Salix arctica* ssp. *crassijulis*	Arctic Willow
_____	*Salix depressa*	Bebb Willow
_____	*Salix glauca*	Grayleaf Willow
_____	*Salix niphoclada*	Barren Ground Willow
_____	*Salix phlebophylla*	Skeleton Leaf Willow
_____	*Salix polaris*	Polar Willow
_____	*Salix reticulata*	Net-leaf Willow
_____	*Salix rotundifolia*	Least Willow
_____	*Salix setchelliana*	Setchell Willow
_____	*Saxifraga bronchialis*	Yellow-spotted Saxifrage
_____	*Saxifraga cernua*	Bulblet Saxifrage
_____	*Saxifraga davurica*	
_____	*Saxifraga eschscholtzii*	Barnacle Saxifrage
_____	*Saxifraga flagellaris*	Spider Saxifrage
_____	*Saxifraga lyallii*	Red-stemmed Saxifrage
_____	*Saxifraga oppositifolia*	Purple Mt. Saxifrage
_____	*Saxifraga punctata* ssp. *nelsoniana*	Brook Saxifrage
_____	*Saxifraga reflexa*	Reflexed Saxifrage
_____	*Saxifraga serpyllifolia*	Thyme-leaf Saxifrage
_____	*Saxifraga tricuspidata*	Prickly Saxifrage
_____	*Sedum rosea*	Dwarf Form Roseroot
_____	*Senecio atropurpureus*	
_____	*Senecio lugens*	Black-tipped Groundsel
_____	*Senecio pauciflorus*	Few-flowered Senecio
_____	*Senecio resedifolius*	Dwarf Arctic Butterweed
_____	*Shepherdia canadensis*	Soapberry
_____	*Silene acaulis* ssp. *acaulis*	Moss Campion
_____	*Silene repens*	Tall Campion
_____	*Smelowskia borealis*	
_____	*Solidago multiradiata*	Northern Goldenrod
_____	*Spiraea beauverdiana*	Alaska Spiraea
_____	*Stellaria alaskanum*	Alaska Starwort
_____	*Stellaria longipes*	Starwort
_____	*Thalictrum alpinum*	Alpine Meadow Rue

_____	*Tofieldia coccinea*	False Asphodel
_____	*Tofieldia pussila*	False Asphodel
_____	*Trientalis europaea*	Star Flower
_____	*Trifolium* sp.	Clover
_____	*Trisetum spicatum*	Alpine Grass
_____	*Vaccinium uliginosum*	Bog Blueberry
_____	*Vaccinium vitis-idaea*	Low-bush Cranberry
_____	*Valeriana capitata*	Capitate Valerian
_____	*Viburnum edule*	High-bush Cranberry
_____	*Viola biflora*	
_____	*Viola selkirkii*	Selkirk's Violet
_____	*Woodsia ilvensis*	Rusty Woodsia
_____	*Zygadenus elegans*	Death Camas

George Parks Highway viewed from Mt. Healy Overlook

Pasque Flower variation

Pasque Flower seed head

Savage River

Included in this list are plants that we saw while hiking up the mountainside on the east side of Savage River, Mile 14.8, (not difficult, although we did not go to the extreme top) and along the trail on the west side of the river (easy). Mostly thicket, wet and dry tundra and stream beds are included in this area. This is good habitat for sheep, arctic ground squirrel and hoary marmot.

Ridge above parking area on east side of Savage River

Playful lamb on the Ridge

Arctic ground squirrel feasting on Alaska Willow leaves while perched in shrub.

_____ *Aconitum delphinifolium* .... Monkshood
_____ *Adoxa moschatellina* .... Muskroot
_____ *Alnus crispa* .... Mountain Alder
_____ *Androsace chamaejasme* .... Rock Jasmine
_____ *Anemone drummondii* .... Blue Anemone
_____ *Anemone narcissiflora* .... Narcissus-flowered Anemone
_____ *Anemone parviflora* .... Windflower
_____ *Anemone richardsonii* .... Yellow Anemone
_____ *Antennaria friesiana* .... White Pussy-toes
_____ *Arabis lyrata* .... Kamchatka Rockcress
_____ *Arctostaphylos alpina* .... Alpine Bearberry
_____ *Arctostaphylos rubra* .... Red Bearberry
_____ *Arctostaphylos uva-ursi* .... Kinnnikinnick
_____ *Arnica frigida* .... Frigid Arnica
_____ *Artemisia arctica* .... Arctic Wormwood
_____ *Artemisia frigida* .... Prairie Sagewort
_____ *Astragalus alpinus* .... Alpine Mild Vetch
_____ *Astragalus umbellatus* .... Hairy Arctic Milk Vetch
_____ *Betula glandulosa* .... Shrub Birch
_____ *Betula nana* .... Dwarf Birch
_____ *Campanula lasiocarpa* ssp. *lasiocarpa* .... Mt. Harebell
_____ *Campanula uniflora* .... One-flowered Harebell
_____ *Cardamine bellidifolia* .... Alpine Bittercress
_____ *Cardamine purpurea* .... Purple Cress
_____ *Cassiope tetragona* .... Bell Heather
_____ *Cerastrium beeringianum* .... Bering Sea Chickweed
_____ *Cornus suecica* .... Lapland Dogwood
_____ *Corydalis pauciflora* .... Few-flowered Corydalis
_____ *Cystopteris fragilis* .... Fragile Fern
_____ *Diapensia lapponica* .... Lapland Diapensia
_____ *Dodecatheon frigidum* .... Frigid Shooting Star
_____ *Draba kamchatica* .... Kamchatka Draba
_____ *Draba longipes* ....
_____ *Draba nivalis* .... Snow Draba
_____ *Dryas integrifolia* .... Entire-leaf Avens
_____ *Dryas octopetala* .... Mountain Avens
_____ *Dryopteris fragrans* .... Fragrant Shield Fern
_____ *Empetrum nigrum* .... Crowberry
_____ *Epilobium angustifolium* .... Common Fireweed
_____ *Epilobium latifolium* .... Dwarf Fireweed
_____ *Equisetum arvense* .... Field Horsetail
_____ *Eriophorum angustifolium* .... Tall Cotton Grass
_____ *Eriophorum scheuchzeri* .... Cotton Grass
_____ *Galium boreale* .... Northern Bedstraw

_____	*Gentiana algida*	Whitish Gentian
_____	*Gentiana glauca*	Glaucous Gentian
_____	*Gentiana propingua*	Four-parted Gentian
_____	*Hedysarum alpinum*	Eskimo Potato
_____	*Hierochloe alpina*	Alpine Holy Grass
_____	*Ledum decumbens*	Narrow-leaf Labrador Tea
_____	*Ligusticum mutellinoides*	Alpine Lovage
_____	*Lloydia serotina*	Alp Lily
_____	*Mertensia paniculata*	Bluebells
_____	*Minuartia arctica*	Arctic Sandwort
_____	*Oxyria digyna*	Mountain Sorrel
_____	*Oxytropis nigresens*	Purple Oxytrope
_____	*Oxytropis viscida*	Sticky Oxytrope
_____	*Parnassia palustris*	Grass of Parnassus
_____	*Parrya nudicaulis* ssp. *interior*	Parry's Wallflower
_____	*Pedicularis capitata*	Capitate Lousewort
_____	*Pedicularis kanei*	Wooly Lousewort
_____	*Pedicularis labradorica*	Labrador Lousewort
_____	*Pedicularis langsdorfii*	Arctic Lousewort
_____	*Pedicularis oederi*	Oederi's Lousewort
_____	*Pedicularis sudetica* ssp. *interior*	Fern Leaf Lousewort
_____	*Petasites frigidus*	Frigid Coltsfoot
_____	*Picea glauca*	White Spruce
_____	*Polemonium acutiflorum*	Tall Jacob's Ladder
_____	*Polygonum bistorta* ssp. *plumosum*	Pink Plumes
_____	*Polygonum viviparum*	Alpine Meadow Bistort
_____	*Populus balsamifera*	Cottonwood
_____	*Populus tremuloides*	Quaking Aspen
_____	*Potentilla biflora*	Two-flowered Cinquefoil
_____	*Potentilla fruticosa*	Tundra Rose
_____	*Potentilla uniflora*	One-flowered Cinquefoil
_____	*Primula egaliksensis*	Greenland Primrose
_____	*Pyrola grandiflora*	Lg. Flowered Pyrola
_____	*Ranunculus nivalis*	Snow Buttercup
_____	*Rhododendron lapponicum*	Lapland Rhododendron
_____	*Ribes triste*	Red Currant
_____	*Rubus arcticus*	Nagoonberry
_____	*Rumex arcticus*	Arctic Dock
_____	*Salix alaxensis*	Alaska Willow
_____	*Salix arctica* ssp. *tortulosa*	Arctic Willow
_____	*Salix barrattiana*	Barratt Willow
_____	*Salix glauca*	Grayleaf Willow
_____	*Salix pulchra*	Diamond Leaf Willow
_____	*Salix reticulata*	Net-leaf Willow

_____ *Salix rotundifolia* .... Least Willow
_____ *Saussurea angustifolia* ....
_____ *Saussurea viscida* ....
_____ *Saxifraga bronchialis* .... Yellow-spotted Saxifrage
_____ *Saxifraga caespitosa* .... Tufted Saxifrage
_____ *Saxifraga cernua* .... Bulblet Saxifrage
_____ *Saxifraga eschscholtzii* .... Barnacle Saxifrage
_____ *Saxifraga hieracifolia* .... Stiff Stem Saxifrage
_____ *Saxifraga hirculus* .... Bog Saxifrage
_____ *Saxifraga oppositifolia* .... Purple Mt. Saxifrage
_____ *Saxifraga punctata* ssp. *nelsoniana* .... Brook Saxifrage
_____ *Saxifraga reflexa* .... Reflexed Saxifrage
_____ *Saxifraga tricuspidata* .... Prickly Saxifrage
_____ *Sedum rosea* ssp. *integrifolium* .... Rosewort
_____ *Senecio fuscatus* ....
_____ *Senecio lugens* .... Black-tipped Groundsel
_____ *Senecio resedifolius* .... Dwarf Arctic Butterweed
_____ *Shepherdia canadensis* .... Soapberry
_____ *Silene acaulis* ssp. *acaulis* .... Moss Campion
_____ *Solidago multiradiata* .... Northern Goldenrod
_____ *Spiraea beauverdiana* .... Alaska Spiraea
_____ *Tofieldia coccinea* .... False Asphodel
_____ *Tofieldia pussila* .... False Asphodel
_____ *Vaccinium uliginosum* .... Bog Blueberry
_____ *Vaccinium vitis-idaea* .... Low-bush Cranberry
_____ *Valeriana capitata* .... Capitate Valerian
_____ *Viola biflora* ....
_____ *Viola epipsila* .... Marsh Violet
_____ *Zygadenus elegans* .... Death Camas

Red fox with arctic ground squirrel---"The Balance of Nature"

Mt. Margaret & Primrose Ridge

Included in this list are the plants that we saw while hiking the mountain and across the ridge. This is a good day hike. Easiest access to the ridge is from a loop pulloff at about mile 17 on the Park road. The ridge starts steeply at Savage River and tapers off to the west end. We encountered thickets, stream beds and wet and dry tundra.

Dry Alpine Tundra---Alpine Bearberry, Blueberry, Low-bush Cranberry and Lichens

Arctic ground squirrel
feasting on Mt. Aven seed heads

Rocky Tundra---top of Mt. Margaret

_____	*Aconitum delphinifolium*	Monkshood
_____	*Alnus crispa*	Mountain Alder
_____	*Anemone narcissiflora*	Narcissus-flowered Anemone
_____	*Anemone parviflora*	Windflower
_____	*Anemone richardsonii*	Yellow Anemone
_____	*Antennaria friesiana*	White Pussy-toes
_____	*Antennaria monocephala*	Cat's Paw
_____	*Arctostaphylos alpina*	Alpine Bearberry
_____	*Arnica frigida*	Frigid Arnica
_____	*Artemisia alaskana*	Alaska Sagebrush
_____	*Artemisia frigida*	Prairie Sagewort
_____	*Artemisia tilesii*	Tall Wormwood
_____	*Aster sibiricus*	Siberian Aster
_____	*Astragalus umbellatus*	Hairy Arctic Milk Vetch
_____	*Betula nana*	Dwarf Birch
_____	*Betula glandulosa*	Shrub Birch
_____	*Betula occidentalis*	Yukon Birch
_____	*Boykinia richardsonii*	Alaska Boykinia
_____	*Campanula lasiocarpa* ssp. *lasiocarpa*	Mt. Harebell
_____	*Cardamine bellidifolia*	Alpine Bittercress
_____	*Cardamine purpurea*	Purple Cress
_____	*Cassiope tetragona*	Bell Heather
_____	*Cerastium beeringianum*	Bering Sea Chickweed
_____	*Cornus suecica*	Lapland Dogwood
_____	*Cystopteris fragilis*	Fragile Fern
_____	*Diapensia lapponica*	Lapland Diapensia
_____	*Dodecatheon frigidum*	Frigid Shooting Star
_____	*Draba hirta*	
_____	*Draba nivalis*	Snow Draba
_____	*Dryas octopetala*	Mountain Avens
_____	*Empetrum nigrum*	Crowberry
_____	*Equisetum arvense*	Field Horsetail
_____	*Gentiana algida*	Whitish Gentian
_____	*Gentiana glauca*	Glaucous Gentian
_____	*Hierochloe alpina*	Alpine Holy Grass
_____	*Lagotis glauca*	Weasel Snout
_____	*Ledum decumbens*	Narrow-leaf Labrador Tea
_____	*Lloydia serotina*	Alp Lily
_____	*Loiseleuria procumbens*	Alpine Azalea
_____	*Melandrium apetalum*	
_____	*Mertensia paniculata*	Bluebells
_____	*Minuartia arctica*	Arctic Sandwort
_____	*Oxytropis maydelliana*	Maydell's Oxytrope
_____	*Oxytropis nigrescens*	Purple Oxytrope
_____	*Papaver macounii*	Macoun's Poppy
_____	*Parnassia kotzebuei*	Small Grass of Parnassus

_____	*Parrya nudicaulis* ssp. *interior*	Parry's Wallflower
_____	*Pedicularis capitata*	Capitate Lousewort
_____	*Pedicularis kanei*	Wooly Lousewort
_____	*Pedicularis labradorica*	Labrador Lousewort
_____	*Pedicularis langsdorfii*	Arctic Lousewort
_____	*Pedicularis oederi*	Oederi's Lousewort
_____	*Petasites frigidus*	Frigid Coltsfoot
_____	*Picea glauca*	White Spruce
_____	*Polemonium acutiflorum*	Tall Jacob's Ladder
_____	*Polygonum bistorta* ssp. *plumosum*	Pink Plumes
_____	*Populus tremuloides*	Quaking Aspen
_____	*Potentilla biflora*	Two-flowered Cinquefoil
_____	*Potentilla hyparctica*	
_____	*Potentilla uniflora*	One-flowered Cinquefoil
_____	*Primula eximia*	
_____	*Primula tschuktschorum*	Chukchi Primrose
_____	*Rhododendron lapponicum*	Lapland Rhododendron
_____	*Rumex arcticus*	Arctic Dock
_____	*Salix alaxensis*	Alaska Willow
_____	*Salix arctica* ssp. *tortulosa*	Arctic Willow
_____	*Salix glauca*	Grayleaf Willow
_____	*Salix phlebophylla*	Skeleton Leaf Willow
_____	*Salix niphoclada*	Barren Ground Willow
_____	*Salix reticulata*	Net-leaf Willow
_____	*Saussurea angustifolia*	
_____	*Saussurea viscida*	
_____	*Saxifraga bronchialis*	Yellow-spotted Saxifrage
_____	*Saxifraga caespitosa*	Tufted Saxifrage
_____	*Saxifraga eschscholtzii*	Barnacle Saxifrage
_____	*Saxifraga hieracifolia*	Stiff Stem Saxifrage
_____	*Saxifraga oppositifolia*	Purple Mt. Saxifrage
_____	*Saxifraga punctata* ssp. *nelsoniana*	Brook Saxifrage
_____	*Saxifraga reflexa*	Reflexed Saxifrage
_____	*Saxifraga serpyllifolia*	Thyme-leaf Saxifrage
_____	*Saxifraga tricuspidata*	Prickly Saxifrage
_____	*Sedum rosea*	Dwarf Form Roseroot
_____	*Sedum rosea* ssp. *integrifolium*	Rosewort
_____	*Senecio atropurpureus*	
_____	*Senecio lugens*	Black-tipped Groundsel
_____	*Silene acaulis* ssp. *acaulis*	Moss Campion
_____	*Spiraea beauverdiana*	Alaska Spiraea
_____	*Stellaria* alaskana	Alaska Starwort
_____	*Stellaria longipes*	Long Stalked Starwort
_____	*Tofieldia coccinea*	False Asphodel
_____	*Vaccinium uliginosum*	Bog Blueberry
_____	*Vaccinium vitis-idaea*	Low-bush Cranberry
_____	*Valeriana capitata*	Capitate Valerian

Cathedral Mt.

Included in this list are plants that we saw while walking up the tundra slopes and back into the riverbed and on some talus slopes about Mile 36. Be reminded that scree and talus slopes can be dangerous if steep or if attempted by inexperienced persons. We did not hike to the top of Cathedral Mountain. The mountain, however, is accessible from both the east and west ends of the ridge. Igloo Mt. has very similar plant life and both areas are favorite habitats for sheep.

Flock of sheep grazing on Mt. Avens.

Mt. Forget-me-nots and Mt. Avens

Smelowskia rosette before blooming, showing how the root pushed the plant out of the ground

_____	*Aconitum delphinifolium*	Monkshood
_____	*Alnus crispa*	Mountain Alder
_____	*Androsace chamaejasme*	Rock Jasmine
_____	*Anemone drummondii*	Blue Anemone
_____	*Anemone narcissiflora*	Narcissus-flowered Anemone
_____	*Anemone parviflora*	Windflower
_____	*Anemone richardsonii*	Yellow Anemone
_____	*Antennaria friesiana*	White Pussy-toes
_____	*Antennaria monocephala*	Cat's Paw
_____	*Arctostaphylos alpina*	Alpine Bearberry
_____	*Arctostaphylos rubra*	Red Bearberry
_____	*Arctostaphylos uva-ursi*	Kinnnikinnick
_____	*Arnica frigida*	Frigid Arnica
_____	*Artemisia alaskana*	Alaska Wormwood
_____	*Artemisia frigida*	Prairie Sagewort
_____	*Artemisia furcata*	
_____	*Artemisia tilesii*	Tall Wormwood
_____	*Astragalus nutzotinensis*	Nootka Milk Vetch
_____	*Astragalus umbellatus*	Hairy Arctic Milk Vetch
_____	*Betula glandulosa*	Shrub Birch
_____	*Boykinia richardsonii*	Alaska Boykinia
_____	*Cardamine purpurea*	Purple Cress
_____	*Cassiope tetragona*	Bell Heather
_____	*Claytonia scammaniana*	Scammen's Spring Beauty
_____	*Crepis nana*	Cushion Hawk's Beard
_____	*Diapensia lapponica*	Lapland Diapensia
_____	*Draba eschscholtzii*	Escholtz's Draba
_____	*Draba hirta*	
_____	*Draba longipes*	
_____	*Draba nivalis*	Snow Draba
_____	*Dryas octopetala*	Mountain Avens
_____	*Empetrum nigrum*	Crowberry
_____	*Epilobium latifolium*	Dwarf Fireweed
_____	*Equisetum arvense*	Field Horsetail
_____	*Erigeron humilis*	Mt. Fleabane
_____	*Erigeron eriocephalus*	
_____	*Eritrichium aretioides*	Mt. Forget-Me-Not
_____	*Erysimum pallasii*	Pallas Wallflower
_____	*Geum rossii*	Ross Avens
_____	*Hedysarum alpinum*	Eskimo Potato
_____	*Hierochloe alpina*	Alpine Holy Grass
_____	*Juniperus communis*	Common Juniper
_____	*Lloydia serotina*	Alp Lily
_____	*Lupinus arcticus*	Arctic Lupine

_____	*Lycopodium selago*	Fir Club Moss
_____	*Mertensia paniculata*	Bluebells
_____	*Minuartia arctica*	Arctic Sandwort
_____	*Oxyria digyna*	Mountain Sorrel
_____	*Oxytropis nigresens*	Purple Oxytrope
_____	*Oxytropis viscida*	Sticky Oxytrope
_____	*Papaver macounii*	Macoun's Poppy
_____	*Parrya nudicaulis* ssp. *interior*	Parry's Wallflower
_____	*Pedicularis capitata*	Capitate Lousewort
_____	*Pedicularis kanei*	Wooly Lousewort
_____	*Petasites frigidus*	Frigid Coltsfoot
_____	*Picea glauca*	White Spruce
_____	*Potentilla fruticosa*	Tundra Rose
_____	*Potentilla uniflora*	One-flowered Cinquefoil
_____	*Pyrola grandiflora*	Lg. Flowered Pyrola
_____	*Rhododendron lapponicum*	Lapland Rhododendron
_____	*Salix alaxensis*	Alaska Willow
_____	*Salix arctica* ssp. *tortulosa*	Arctic Willow
_____	*Salix niphoclada*	Barren Ground Willow
_____	*Salix reticulata*	Net-leaf Willow
_____	*Saussurea angustifolia*	
_____	*Saxifraga cernua*	Bulblet Saxifrage
_____	*Saxifraga reflexa*	Reflexed Saxifrage
_____	*Saxifraga tricuspidata*	Prickly Saxifrage
_____	*Sedum rosea* ssp. *integrifolium*	Rosewort
_____	*Senecio resedifolius*	Dwarf Arctic Butterweed
_____	*Shepherdia canadensis*	Soapberry
_____	*Silene acaulis* ssp. *acaulis*	Moss Campion
_____	*Smelowskia borealis*	
_____	*Solidago multiradiata*	Northern Goldenrod
_____	*Stellaria* longipes	Long Stalked Starwort
_____	*Tofieldia coccinea*	False Asphodel
_____	*Vaccinium uliginosum*	Bog Blueberry
_____	*Zygadenus elegans*	Death Camas

Shrub Birch (Thorofare River)

Polychrome Rest Area

Included in this list are plants easily seen on easy walks from the Rest Area at Mile 45.9. Because this area is used by so many people, visitors are required to stay on the marked trails when close to the Rest Area to prevent damage to the delicate alpine tundra. We did take a side trip down to a small lake beyond the overlook. If you are travelling in a private vehicle you are <u>not</u> allowed to stop at the Rest Area. You would need to drive about 1 /2 mile farther west, where there is a large safe pull-off in which to park your vehicle off the roadway. Most plants seen here, however, were seen in other parts of the Park.

View from Polychrome Rest Area---Dwarf Birch (red), Dwarf Willow (yellow)

Spring Beauty   Purple Mountain Saxifrage
            (Polychrome Mt., Backcountry)

_____	*Aconitum delphinifolium*	Monkshood
_____	*Androsace chamaejasme*	Rock Jasmine
_____	*Anemone narcissiflora*	Narcissus-flowered Anemone
_____	*Anemone parviflora*	Windflower
_____	*Anemone richardsonii*	Yellow Anemone
_____	*Antennaria friesiana*	White Pussy-toes
_____	*Antennaria monocephala*	Cat's Paw
_____	*Arnica frigida*	Frigid Arnica
_____	*Artemisia alaskana*	Alaska Sagebrush
_____	*Artemisia arctica*	Arctic Wormwood
_____	*Astragalus alpinus*	Alpine Mild Vetch
_____	*Betula glandulosa*	Shrub Birch
_____	*Boykinia richardsonii*	Alaska Boykinia
_____	*Caltha palustris* ssp. *arctica*	Marsh Marigold
_____	*Cardamine purpurea*	Purple Cress
_____	*Cassiope tetragona*	Bell Heather
_____	*Chrysosplenium tetrandrum*	Northern Water Carpet
_____	*Claytonia sarmentosa*	Spring Beauty
_____	*Claytonia scammaniana*	Scammen's Spring Beauty
_____	*Corydalis pauciflora*	Few-flowered Corydalis
_____	*Diapensia lapponica*	Lapland Diapensia
_____	*Dodecatheon frigidum*	Frigid Shooting Star
_____	*Douglasia gormanii*	Douglasia
_____	*Draba longipes*	
_____	*Draba nivalis*	Snow Draba
_____	*Dryas octopetala*	Mountain Avens
_____	*Empetrum nigrum*	Crowberry
_____	*Epilobium angustifolium*	Common Fireweed
_____	*Epilobium latifolium*	Dwarf Fireweed
_____	*Erysimum pallasii*	Pallas Wallflower
_____	*Gentiana algida*	Whitish Gentian
_____	*Gentiana glauca*	Glaucous Gentian
_____	*Hedysarum alpinum*	Eskimo Potato
_____	*Hierochloe alpina*	Alpine Holy Grass
_____	*Ledum decumbens*	Narrow-leaf Labrador Tea
_____	*Ligusticum mutellinoides*	Alpine Lovage
_____	*Lloydia serotina*	Alp Lily
_____	*Lycopodium selago*	Fir Club Moss
_____	*Mertensia paniculata*	Bluebells
_____	*Minuartia arctica*	Arctic Sandwort
_____	*Myosotis alpestris* ssp. *asiatica*	Alpine Forget-Me-Not
_____	*Oxytropis nigresens*	Purple Oxytrope
_____	*Oxytropis viscida*	Sticky Oxytrope
_____	*Papaver lapponicum*	Lapland Poppy

_____	*Parrya nudicaulis* ssp. *interior*	Parry's Wallflower
_____	*Pedicularis capitata*	Capitate Lousewort
_____	*Pedicularis kanei*	Wooly Lousewort
_____	*Pedicularis labradorica*	Labrador Lousewort
_____	*Petasites frigidus*	Frigid Coltsfoot
_____	*Polemonium acutiflorum*	Tall Jacob's Ladder
_____	*Polygonum bistorta* ssp. *plumosum*	Pink Plumes
_____	*Potentilla fruticosa*	Tundra Rose
_____	*Potentilla uniflora*	One-flowered Cinquefoil
_____	*Pyrola grandiflora*	Lg. Flowered Pyrola
_____	*Rhododendron lapponicum*	Lapland Rhododendron
_____	*Rumex arcticus*	Arctic Dock
_____	*Salix arctica* ssp. *tortulosa*	Arctic Willow
_____	*Salix niphoclada*	Barren Ground Willow
_____	*Salix pulchra*	Diamond Leaf Willow
_____	*Salix reticulata*	Net-leaf Willow
_____	*Saussurea angustifolia*	
_____	*Saxifraga bronchialis*	Yellow-spotted Saxifrage
_____	*Saxifraga cernua*	Bulblet Saxifrage
_____	*Saxifraga eschscholtzii*	Barnacle Saxifrage
_____	*Saxifraga hieracifolia*	Stiff Stem Saxifrage
_____	*Saxifraga hirculus*	Bog Saxifrage
_____	*Saxifraga punctata* ssp. *nelsoniana*	Brook Saxifrage
_____	*Saxifraga reflexa*	Reflexed Saxifrage
_____	*Saxifraga tricuspidata*	Prickly Saxifrage
_____	*Sedum rosea* ssp. *integrifolium*	Rosewort
_____	*Senecio atropurpureus*	
_____	*Senecio fuscatus*	
_____	*Senecio resedifolius*	Dwarf Arctic Butterweed
_____	*Shepherdia canadensis*	Soapberry
_____	*Silene acaulis* ssp. *acaulescens*	Moss Campion
_____	*Vaccinium uliginosum*	Bog Blueberry
_____	*Vaccinium vitis-idaea*	Low-bush Cranberry
_____	*Valeriana capitata*	Capitate Valerian
_____	*Viola biflora*	
_____	*Woodsia ilvensis*	Rusty Woodsia

Eielson Visitor Center and Thoro Ridge

Included in this list are plants easily seen while walking around the Eielson Visitor Center, Mile 66, or on a strenuous hike up Thoro Ridge (across the road from the Visitor Center). The main habitats encountered here are dry tundra, scree, and some talus. This is a favored spot of grizzly bear, caribou, red fox and arctic ground squirrel.

Scamman's Spring Beauty (Thoro Ridge)

Eielson Visitor Center
(from Thoro Ridge)

"Reshaping of Tundra"
(caused by soil erosion in the spring)

_____	*Aconitum delphinifolium*	Monkshood
_____	*Alnus crispa*	Mountain Alder
_____	*Androsace chamaejasme*	Rock Jasmine
_____	*Anemone drummondii*	Blue Anemone
_____	*Anemone narcissiflora*	Narcissus-flowered Anemone
_____	*Anemone parviflora*	Windflower
_____	*Anemone richardsonii*	Yellow Anemone
_____	*Angelica lucida*	Wild Celery
_____	*Antennaria friesiana*	White Pussy-toes
_____	*Antennaria monocephala*	Cat's Paw
_____	*Arctostaphylos alpina*	Alpine Bearberry
_____	*Arenaria chamissonis*	
_____	*Arnica frigida*	Frigid Arnica
_____	*Arnica lessingii*	Lessing's Arnica
_____	*Artemisia arctica*	Arctic Wormwood
_____	*Artemisia furcata*	
_____	*Artemisia tilesii*	Tall Wormwood
_____	*Aster sibiricus*	Siberian Aster
_____	*Astragalus umbellatus*	Hairy Arctic Milk Vetch
_____	*Betula nana*	Dwarf Birch
_____	*Botrychium boreale*	Northern moonwort
_____	*Campanula lasiocarpa* ssp. *lasiocarpa*	Mt. Harebell
_____	*Cardamine bellidifolia*	Alpine Bittercress
_____	*Carex nardina*	
_____	*Cassiope tetragona*	Bell Heather
_____	*Cerastium beeringianum*	Bering Sea Chickweed
_____	*Claytonia acutifolia*	Bering Sea Spring Beauty
_____	*Claytonia sarmentosa*	Alaska Spring Beauty
_____	*Claytonia scammaniana*	Scammen's Spring Beauty
_____	*Claytonia tuberosa*	Tuberous Spring Beauty
_____	*Coeloglossum viride*	Frog Orchid
_____	*Diapensia lapponica*	Lapland Diapensia
_____	*Dodecatheon frigidum*	Frigid Shooting Star
_____	*Dryas octopetala*	Mountain Avens
_____	*Empetrum nigrum*	Crowberry
_____	*Epilobium angustifolium*	Common Fireweed
_____	*Epilobium latifolium*	Dwarf Fireweed
_____	*Epilobium* sp.	Willow Herbs
_____	*Equisetum arvense*	Field Horsetail
_____	*Erigeron humilis*	Mt. Fleabane
_____	*Erigeron eriocephalus*	
_____	*Erigeron purpuratus*	
_____	*Eriophorum angustifolium*	Tall Cotton Grass
_____	*Galium boreale*	Northern Bedstraw
_____	*Gentiana algida*	Whitish Gentian

	Scientific Name	Common Name
_____	*Gentiana glauca*	Glaucous Gentian
_____	*Gentiana propingua*	Four-parted Gentian
_____	*Geranium erianthum*	Wild Geranium
_____	*Hedysarum alpinum*	Eskimo Potato
_____	*Juncus mertensianus*	Merten's Rush
_____	*Lagotis glauca*	Weasel Snout
_____	*Ledum decumbens*	Narrow-leaf Labrador Tea
_____	*Ligusticum mutellinoides*	Alpine Lovage
_____	*Lloydia serotina*	Alp Lily
_____	*Loiseleuria procumbens*	Alpine Azalea
_____	*Lupinus arcticus*	Arctic Lupine
_____	*Melandrium apetalum*	Bluebells
_____	*Mertensia paniculata*	Bluebells
_____	*Minuartia arctica*	Arctic Sandwort
_____	*Minuartia rossii*	
_____	*Moehringia lateriflora*	Grove Sandwort
_____	*Oxyria digyna*	Mountain Sorrel
_____	*Oxytropis deflexa* ssp. *foliolosa*	
_____	*Oxytropis maydelliana*	Maydell's Oxytrope
_____	*Oxytropis nigresens*	Purple Oxytrope
_____	*Oxytropis scammaniana*	Scamman's Oxytrope
_____	*Papaver alaskanum*	Alaska Poppy
_____	*Papaver lapponicum*	Lapland Poppy
_____	*Papaver macounii*	Macoun's Poppy
_____	*Parrya nudicaulis* ssp. interior	Parry's Wallflower
_____	*Pedicularis capitata*	Capitate Lousewort
_____	*Pedicularis kanei*	Wooly Lousewort
_____	*Pedicularis oederi*	Oederi's Lousewort
_____	*Pedicularis verticillata*	Whorled-leaf Lousewort
_____	*Petasites frigidus*	Frigid Coltsfoot
_____	*Platanthera hyperborea*	Northern Green Bog Orchid
_____	*Polygonum bistorta* ssp. *plumosum*	Pink Plumes
_____	*Podistera macounii*	
_____	*Polygonum viviparum*	Alpine Meadow Bistort
_____	*Potentilla fruticosa*	Tundra Rose
_____	*Potentilla hyparctica*	
_____	*Potentilla uniflora*	One-flowered Cinquefoil
_____	*Primula eximia*	
_____	*Primula tschuktschorum*	Chukchi Primrose
_____	*Ranunculus eschscholtzii*	Eschscholtz's Buttercup
_____	*Ranunculus gelidus*	
_____	*Rhododendron lapponicum*	Lapland Rhododendron
_____	*Rubus arcticus*	Nagoonberry
_____	*Rumex acetosa*	Meadow Sheep Sorrel
_____	*Salix alaxensis*	Alaska Willow

_____	*Salix arctica* ssp. *torulosa*	Arctic Willow
_____	*Salix barrattiana*	Barratt Willow
_____	*Salix phlebophylla*	Skeleton Leaf Willow
_____	*Salix reticulata*	Net-leaf Willow
_____	*Salix rotundifolia*	Least Willow
_____	*Sanguisorba stipulata*	Sitka Burnet
_____	*Saussurea angustifolia*	
_____	*Saussurea viscida*	
_____	*Saxifraga bronchialis*	Yellow-spotted Saxifrage
_____	*Saxifraga flagellaris*	Spider Saxifrage
_____	*Saxifraga nelsoniana*	Brook Saxifrage
_____	*Saxifraga oppositifolia*	Purple Mt. Saxifrage
_____	*Saxifraga punctata* ssp. *nelsoniana*	Brook Saxifrage
_____	*Saxifraga reflexa*	Reflexed Saxifrage
_____	*Saxifraga serpyllifolia*	Thyme-leaf Saxifrage
_____	*Sedum rosea* ssp. *integrifolium*	Rosewort
_____	*Senecio atropurpureus*	
_____	*Senecio fuscatus*	
_____	*Senecio lugens*	Black-tipped Groundsel
_____	*Senecio resedifolius*	Dwarf Arctic Butterweed
_____	*Sibbaldia procumbens*	
_____	*Silene acaulis* ssp. *acaulis*	Moss Campion
_____	*Smelowskia borealis*	
_____	*Solidago multiradiata*	Northern Goldenrod
_____	*Spiraea beauverdiana*	Alaska Spiraea
_____	*Stellaria alaskanum*	Alaska Starwort
_____	*Stellaria monantha*	Starwort
_____	*Taraxacum kamtschaticum*	Kamchatka Dandelion
_____	*Thalictrum alpinum*	Alpine Meadow Rue
_____	*Tofieldia coccinea*	False Asphodel
_____	*Vaccinium uliginosum*	Bog Blueberry
_____	*Vaccinium vitis-idaea*	Low-bush Cranberry
_____	*Valeriana capitata*	Capitate Valerian
_____	*Veronica wormskjoldii*	Alpine Veronica
_____	*Viola biflora*	
_____	*Viola epipsila*	Marsh Violet
_____	*Zygadenus elegans*	Death Camas

Wonder Lake and McKinley River Bar Trail

Included in this list are plants that we observed while hiking the Wonder Lake Campground Road, Mile 84.6, and along the McKinley River Bar Trail. This trail starts from a trailhead sign about 1/2 mile before the Wonder Lake Campground on the Campground Road. This trail is very wet and requires stream crossings and walking through bogs --- waterproof boots or rubber knee boots are recommended. Bear, moose, caribou and wolves might be seen in these areas.

Dwarf Dogwood---fall color (McKinley River Bar Trail)

Wilhelmsia (McKinley River Bar Trail)

Tufted Cotton Grass (Wonder Lake)

False Asphodel (McKinley River Bar Trail)

_____	*Aconitum delphinifolium*	Monkshood
_____	*Alnus crispa*	Mountain Alder
_____	*Andromeda polifolia*	Bog Rosemary
_____	*Anemone narcissiflora*	Narcissus-flowered Anemone
_____	*Anemone parviflora*	Windflower
_____	*Anemone richardsonii*	Yellow Anemone
_____	*Antennaria friesiana*	White Pussy-toes
_____	*Antennaria pallida*	
_____	*Arctostaphylos alpina*	Alpine Bearberry
_____	*Arctostaphylos rubra*	Red Bearberry
_____	*Arnica frigida*	Frigid Arnica
_____	*Arnica lessingii*	Lessing's Arnica
_____	*Artemisia arctica*	Arctic Wormwood
_____	*Artemisia tilesii*	Tall Wormwood
_____	*Aster sibiricus*	Siberian Aster
_____	*Astragalus alpinus*	Alpine Mild Vetch
_____	*Astragalus umbellatus*	Hairy Arctic Milk Vetch
_____	*Betula glandulosa*	Shrub Birch
_____	*Betula nana*	Dwarf Birch
_____	*Betula occidentalis*	Yukon Birch
_____	*Boschniakia rossica*	Broom Rape
_____	*Campanula lasiocarpa* ssp. *lasiocarpa*	Mt. Harebell
_____	*Cardamine pratensis*	Cuckoo Flower
_____	*Cerastrium arvense*	Mouse-ear Chickweed
_____	*Cornus canadensis*	Canadian Dwarf Dogwood
_____	*Cornus suecica*	Lapland Dogwood
_____	*Dodecatheon frigidum*	Frigid Shooting Star
_____	*Drosera rotundifolia*	Round-leaf Sundew
_____	*Dryas drummondii*	Yellow Dryas
_____	*Dryas integrifolia*	Entire-leaf Avens
_____	*Dryas octopetala*	Mountain Avens
_____	*Empetrum nigrum*	Crowberry
_____	*Epilobium angustifolium*	Common Fireweed
_____	*Epilobium latifolium*	Dwarf Fireweed
_____	*Equisetum scirpoides*	
_____	*Equisetum silvaticum*	Woodland Horsetail
_____	*Erigeron lonchophyllus*	Long Leaf Fleabane
_____	*Eriophorum angustifolium*	Tall Cotton Grass
_____	*Eriophorum vaginatum*	Tufted Cotton Grass
_____	*Galium boreale*	Northern Bedstraw
_____	*Geum macrophyllum*	Large-leaf Avens
_____	*Hedysarum alpinum*	Eskimo Potato
_____	*Heracleum lanatum*	Cow Parsnip
_____	*Ledum decumbens*	Narrow-leaf Labrador Tea
_____	*Ledum palustre*	Labrador Tea

_____	*Linnaea borealis*	Twinflower
_____	*Loiseleuria procumbens*	Alpine Azalea
_____	*Luzula parviflora*	Few-flowered Wood Rush
_____	*Lycopodium annotinum*	Stiff Club Moss
_____	*Lycopodium complanatum*	Creeping Jenny
_____	*Mertensia paniculata*	Bluebells
_____	*Moehringia lateriflora*	Grove Sandwort
_____	*Oxycoccus microcarpus*	Bog Cranberry
_____	*Oxytropis campestris*	Field Oxytrope
_____	*Oxytropis maydelliana*	Maydell's Oxytrope
_____	*Parnassia kotzebuei*	Small Grass of Parnassus
_____	*Parnassia palustris*	Grass of Parnassus
_____	*Pedicularis capitata*	Capitate Lousewort
_____	*Pedicularis labradorica*	Labrador Lousewort
_____	*Pedicularis oederi*	Oederi's Lousewort
_____	*Pedicularis sudetica* ssp. *interior*	Fern Leaf Lousewort
_____	*Pedicularis verticillata*	Whorled-leaf Lousewort
_____	*Petasites frigidus*	Frigid Coltsfoot
_____	*Picea glauca*	White Spruce
_____	*Pinguicula villosa*	Small Butterwort
_____	*Plantago major*	Common Plantain
_____	*Platanthera hyperborea*	Mt. Green Bog Orchid
_____	*Platanthera obtusata*	One-leaf Rein Orchid
_____	*Poa alpina*	Alpine Blue Grass
_____	*Polemonium acutiflorum*	Tall Jacob's Ladder
_____	*Polygonum alaskanum*	Wild Rhubarb
_____	*Polygonum bistorta* ssp. *plumosum*	Pink Plumes
_____	*Polygonum viviparum*	Alpine Meadow Bistort
_____	*Populus balsamifera*	Cottonwood
_____	*Populus tremuloides*	Quaking Aspen
_____	*Potentilla fruticosa*	Tundra Rose
_____	*Potentilla norvegica* ssp. *monspeliens*	Norwegian Cinquefoil
_____	*Pyrola asarifolia*	Pink Pyrola
_____	*Pyrola grandiflora*	Large Flowered Pyrola
_____	*Pyrola minor*	Small Flowered Pyrola
_____	*Pyrola secunda*	Sidebells Pyrola
_____	*Rosa acicularis*	Prickly Rose
_____	*Rubus arcticus*	Nagoonberry
_____	*Rubus chamaemorus*	Cloudberry
_____	*Rubus idaeus*	Raspberry
_____	*Rumex acetosa*	Meadow Sheep Sorrel
_____	*Rumex arcticus*	Arctic Dock
_____	*Salix alaxensis*	Alaska Willow

	Salix arctica ssp. tortulosa	Arctic Willow
	Salix barclayii	Barclay Willow
	Salix depressa	Bebb Willow
	Salix glauca	Grayleaf Willow
	Salix niphoclada	Barren Ground Willow
	Salix pulchra	Diamond Leaf Willow
	Salix reticulata	Net-leaf Willow
	Sanguisorba officinalis	Red Burnet
	Sanguisorba stipulata	Sitka Burnet
	Saussurea angustifolia	
	Sedum rosea ssp. *integrifolium*	Rosewort
	Senecio lugens	Black-tipped Groundsel
	Shepherdia canadensis	Soapberry
	Solidago multiradiata	Northern Goldenrod
	Spiraea beauverdiana	Alaska Spiraea
	Tofieldia coccinea	False Asphodel
	Tofieldia pussila	False Asphodel
	Trientalis europaea	Star Flower
	Triglochin palustris	Arrow Grass
	Vaccinium uliginosum	Bog Blueberry
	Vaccinium vitis-idaea	Low-bush Cranberry
	Valeriana capitata	Capitate Valerian
	Viola epipsila	Marsh Violet
	Zygadenus elegans	Death Camas

Wonder Lake from Camp Ridge (behind North Face Lodge)

"Inholdings" Lodges

Beyond Wonder Lake Ranger Station are private "inholdings" land within the new National Park & Preserve (added in 1990). In addition to many patented and unpatented mining claims are 3 private lodges: Camp Denali/North Face Lodge, the Kantishna Roadhouse, and the Denali Backcountry Lodge. These establishments offer a pleasant place to stay, excellent food and activities, including wildflower walks, for their guests.

Camp Denali / North Face Lodge

Kantishna Roadhouse

Quigley Ridge and Wickersham Dome

Included in this list are plants that we observed while on hikes from Kantishna Roadhouse. Although this area is open to everyone, these areas are probably used mostly by guests of the lodges in Kantishna. They are about 5 miles beyond Wonder Lake and there are many other areas to explore in the Park that are more accessible. This is easy hiking on an old mining road up into alpine areas.

Parry's Wallflower, Wind Flower, Frigid Shooting Star

Hoary Marmot on alert

Scamman's Oxytrope (Wickersham Dome)

_____ *Aconitum delphinifolium* .... Monkshood
_____ *Adoxa moschatellina* .... Muskroot
_____ *Alnus crispa* .... Mountain Alder
_____ *Androsace chamaejasme* .... Rock Jasmine
_____ *Anemone narcissiflora* .... Narcissus-flowered Anemone
_____ *Anemone parviflora* .... Windflower
_____ *Anemone richardsonii* .... Yellow Anemone
_____ *Angelica lucida* .... Wild Celery
_____ *Antennaria friesiana* .... White Pussy-toes
_____ *Antennaria isolepis* ....
_____ *Antennaria monocephala* .... Cat's Paw
_____ *Arabis lyrata* .... Kamchatka Rockcress
_____ *Arctostaphylos alpina* .... Alpine Bearberry
_____ *Arnica frigida* .... Frigid Arnica
_____ *Arnica lessingii* .... Lessing's Arnica
_____ *Artemisia arctica* .... Arctic Wormwood
_____ *Artemisia tilesii* .... Tall Wormwood
_____ *Aster sibiricus* .... Siberian Aster
_____ *Astragalus umbellatus* .... Hairy Arctic Milk Vetch
_____ *Betula glandulosa* .... Shrub Birch
_____ *Betula nana* .... Dwarf Birch
_____ *Betula occidentalis* .... Yukon Birch
_____ *Betula papyrifera* .... Paper Birch
_____ *Boschniakia rossica* .... Broom Rape
_____ *Boykinia richardsonii* .... Alaska Boykinia
_____ *Bupleurum triradiatum* .... Thoroughwort
_____ *Campanula lasiocarpa* ssp. *lasiocarpa* .... Mt. Harebell
_____ *Cardamine pratensis* .... Cuckoo Flower
_____ *Cardamine purpurea* .... Purple Cress
_____ *Carex scirpoidea* .... Sedge
_____ *Cassiope tetragona* .... Bell Heather
_____ *Castilleja elegans* .... Elegant Paintbrush
_____ *Chrysosplenium tetrandrum* .... Northern Water Carpet
_____ *Claytonia sarmentosa* .... Spring Beauty
_____ *Coeloglossum viride* .... Frog Orchid
_____ *Cornus suecica* .... Lapland Dogwood
_____ *Corydalis pauciflora* .... Few-flowered Corydalis
_____ *Cystopteris fragilis* .... Fragile Fern
_____ *Diapensia lapponica* .... Lapland Diapensia
_____ *Dodecatheon frigidum* .... Frigid Shooting Star
_____ *Draba hirta* ....
_____ *Draba longipes* ....
_____ *Dryas octopetala* .... Mountain Avens
_____ *Dryopteris fragrans* .... Fragrant Shield Fern

_____	*Empetrum nigrum*	Crowberry
_____	*Epilobium angustifolium*	Common Fireweed
_____	*Epilobium latifolium*	Dwarf Fireweed
_____	*Epilobium* sp.	Willow Herbs
_____	*Equisetum arvense*	Field Horsetail
_____	*Eriophorum angustifolium*	Tall Cotton Grass
_____	*Galium boreale*	Northern Bedstraw
_____	*Gentiana algida*	Whitish Gentian
_____	*Gentiana glauca*	Glaucous Gentian
_____	*Gentiana prostrata*	Moss Gentian
_____	*Geocaulon lividum*	Timberberry
_____	*Geranium erianthum*	Wild Geranium
_____	*Hedysarum alpinum*	Eskimo Potato
_____	*Heracleum lanatum*	Cow Parsnip
_____	*Juniperus communis*	Common Juniper
_____	*Ledum decumbens*	Narrow-leaf Labrador Tea
_____	*Ledum palustre*	Labrador Tea
_____	*Ligusticum mutellinoides*	Alpine Lovage
_____	*Linnaea borealis*	Twinflower
_____	*Lloydia serotina*	Alp Lily
_____	*Loiseleuria procumbens*	Alpine Azalea
_____	*Lupinus arcticus*	Arctic Lupine
_____	*Mertensia paniculata*	Bluebells
_____	*Minuartia arctica*	Arctic Sandwort
_____	*Moehringia lateriflora*	Grove Sandwort
_____	*Myosotis alpestris* ssp. *asiatica*	Alpine Forget-Me-Not
_____	*Oxyria digyna*	Mountain Sorrel
_____	*Oxytropis maydelliana*	Maydell's Oxytrope
_____	*Oxytropis nigresens*	Purple Oxytrope
_____	*Papaver macounii*	Macoun's Poppy
_____	*Parnassia palustris*	Grass of Parnassus
_____	*Parrya nudicaulis* ssp. *interior*	Parry's Wallflower
_____	*Pedicularis capitata*	Capitate Lousewort
_____	*Pedicularis kanei*	Wooly Lousewort
_____	*Pedicularis labradorica*	Labrador Lousewort
_____	*Pedicularis oederi*	Oederi's Lousewort
_____	*Pedicularis sudetica* ssp. *interior*	Fern Leaf Lousewort
_____	*Pedicularis verticillata*	Whorled-leaf Lousewort
_____	*Petasites frigidus*	Frigid Coltsfoot
_____	*Picea glauca*	White Spruce
_____	*Plantago major*	Common Plantain
_____	*Polemonium acutiflorum*	Tall Jacob's Ladder
_____	*Polygonum alaskanum*	Wild Rhubarb
_____	*Polygonum bistorta* ssp. *plumosum*	Pink Plumes
_____	*Polygonum viviparum*	Alpine Meadow Bistort

_____	*Populus balsamifera*	Cottonwood
_____	*Populus tremuloides*	Quaking Aspen
_____	*Potentilla fruticosa*	Tundra Rose
_____	*Potentilla uniflora*	One-flowered Cinquefoil
_____	*Primula cuneifolia*	Pixie Eye Primrose
_____	*Pyrola asarifolia*	Pink Pyrola
_____	*Pyrola minor*	Small Flowered Pyrola
_____	*Pyrola secunda*	Sidebells Pyrola
_____	*Ranunculus nivalis*	Snow Buttercup
_____	*Rhododendron lapponicum*	Lapland Rhododendron
_____	*Ribes triste*	Red Currant
_____	*Rosa acicularis*	Prickly Rose
_____	*Rubus arcticus*	Nagoonberry
_____	*Rubus chamaemorus*	Cloudberry
_____	*Rubus idaeus*	Raspberry
_____	*Salix alaxensis*	Alaska Willow
_____	*Salix arctica* ssp. *tortulosa*	Arctic Willow
_____	*Salix depressa*	Bebb Willow
_____	*Salix glauca*	Gray Leaf Willow
_____	*Salix pulcha*	Diamond Leaf Willow
_____	*Sanguisorba stipulata*	Sitka Burnet
_____	*Saussurea angustifolia*	
_____	*Saxifraga bronchialis*	Yellow-spotted Saxifrage
_____	*Saxifraga cernua*	Bulblet Saxifrage
_____	*Saxifraga eschscholtzii*	Barnacle Saxifrage
_____	*Saxifraga hiercifolia*	Stiff Stem Saxifrage
_____	*Saxifraga nelsoniana*	Brook Saxifrage
_____	*Saxifraga oppositifolia*	Purple Mt. Saxifrage
_____	*Saxifraga punctata* ssp. *nelsoniana*	Brook Saxifrage
_____	*Saxifraga reflexa*	Reflexed Saxifrage
_____	*Saxifraga tricuspidata*	Prickly Saxifrage
_____	*Sedum rosea*	Dwarf Form Roseroot
_____	*Senecio atropurpureus*	
_____	*Senecio lugens*	Black-tipped Groundsel
_____	*Silene acaulis* ssp. *acaulis*	Moss Campion
_____	*Solidago multiradiata*	Northern Goldenrod
_____	*Spiraea beauverdiana*	Alaska Spiraea
_____	*Thalictrum alpinum*	Alpine Meadow Rue
_____	*Tofieldia coccinea*	False Asphodel
_____	*Tofieldia pussila*	False Asphodel
_____	*Vaccinium uliginosum*	Bog Blueberry
_____	*Vaccinium vitis-idaea*	Low-bush Cranberry
_____	*Valeriana capitata*	Capitate Valerian
_____	*Veronica wormskjoldii*	Alpine Veronica
_____	*Viola biflora*	
_____	*Viola epipsila*	Marsh Violet
_____	*Woodsia glabella*	Smooth Woodsia
_____	*Zygadenus elegans*	Death Camas

Poisonous Plants

ALL ANEMONES (*Anemone* species)--All contain poisonous anemonin, very dangerous.

BOG ROSEMARY (*Andromeda polifolia*)--Contains Andromedotoxin--causes lowered blood pressure, difficult breathing, vomiting, diarrhea and cramps. At one time it was used medicinally with careful control.

BUTTERCUP (*Ranunculus* species)--For emergency food use, poison can be broken down by boiling and changes of water until bitter taste is gone.

DEATH CAMAS (*Zygadenus elegans*)--Very poisonous. Extremely bitter. Death results from respiratory depression and asphyxia.

FIR CLUB MOSS (*Lycopodium selago*)--Contains a poisonous alkaloid causing pain in the mouth, vomiting and diarrhea.

LABRADOR TEA (*Ledum palustre*)---Reports of cathartic effect if too much tea is consumed. The robustly aromatic leaves make it one of the most famous teas in the North Country.

LARKSPUR (*Delphinium* species)--Poisonous like Monkshood, but not quite as active.

LUPINE (*Lupinus* species)--Leaves and seeds poisonous.

MARSH MARIGOLD (*Caltha palustris*)--Raw plant is poisonous. Poison is broken down by boiling.

MONKSHOOD (*Aconitum* species)--All parts poisonous. Once called Wolfbane. Was once used as a spear or arrow poison because it contains a neurotoxin that would paralyze animals without affecting edibility of the meat.

WILD SWEET PEA (*Hedysarum mackenzii*)--Edibility very questionable, possibly poisonous.

IMPORTANT NOTES:

1) The fact that a certain plant is edible by animals and/or birds does not guarantee that it is edible by humans; in fact, it may be extremely toxic to humans because of differences in the digestive systems.

2) Impress upon your family and friends to never eat any unknown plant or berry.

3) In case of poisoning, contact medical personnel and be prepared to tell them the name of the plant involved or give an accurate description. Better to be safe, even if embarrassed, than sorry!

4) Remember, it takes less poison to be fatal to a small child than for an adult.

PLANT FAMILY CHARACTERISTICS

Plants are divided into families by differences of reproductive parts; such as, number and placement of stamens, how the ovaries are divided, placement of seeds within the ovaries, manner of seed dispersement, etc. However, these characteristics are not always available or easily noticed, so I have listed below some other, more obvious, characteristics to look for. In botany, there are a lot of "usually"'s, some families vary greatly, and many oddities do occur. Included here are the families that we observed.

(1) Aster / Asteraceae---formerly the daisy or Composite/ Compositae. Herbaceous plants or shrubs having a head of flowers (composed of many flowers), usually disk flowers, surrounded by showy ray flowers (sometimes incorrectly called petals) with a circle of bracts at the base. Leaf shape and placement variable according to genus.

(2) Bladderwort / Lentibulareaceae---insectivorous plants of wet areas having irregularly shaped flowers with 2 to 5 sepals, 5 united petals, and 2 stamens. Terrestrial plants have a rosette of leaves, while aquatic varieties have finely dissected leaves on long, floating stems.

(3) Bluebell / Campanulaceae---herbaceous plants with a few flowers having 5 sepals, 5 petals (united at base and, frequently, bell-shaped), 5 stamens, and 1 ovary. Leaves are simple and alternate on stems.

(4) Borage / Boraginaceae---herbaceous plants with branched stems with many flowers having 5 united sepals, 5 united petals (bell-shaped or salverform), 5 stamens, and an ovary divided into 2 parts (often times lobed, giving the appearance of 4 parts). Leaves are alternate, simple, usually hairy and frequently the buds are in a curled cyme.

(5) Buckwheat / Polygonaceae---herbaceous plants with a spike of many small flowers having 5 sepals, no petals; and, usually, 8 stamens. Leaves are simple, sometimes basal, but usually on the stem.

(6) Buttercup or Crowfoot / Ranunculaceae---herbaceous plants with 1 to many common flowers usually having 5 sepals, 5 petals, many stamens (tight cushion effect). This is a very variable family having unusual numbers of petals or sepals; and, sometimes completely lacking petals. Leaves are frequently divided into a lobed or dissected crowfoot (birdfoot) pattern, have long stems, and are predominantly basal. Many members of this family are poisonous.

(7) Crowberry / Empetraceae---evergreen shrubs having inconspicuous flowers of 3 bracts, 3 to 6 sepals (sometimes in whorls and confused as petals) and 2 to 4 stamens. The ovary is divided into many parts and produces a round, black berry. Leaves are simple and heath-like.

(8) Diapensia / Diapensiaceae---evergreen shrubs having flowers with 5 sepals, 5 united petals, 5 stamens, and the ovary divided into 3 sections. Leaves are very small. There is one alpine member in Alaska.

(9) Dogwood / Cornaceae---shrubs or sub-shrubs having clusters of very small flowers consisting of 4 showy bracts, 4 sepals, 4 petals, 4 stamens, and 1 ovary which produces a soft berry. The 4 large, showy bracts are often confused with petals. The simple leaves have arcuate veins.

(10) Earthsmoke / Fumariaceae---herbaceous plants having delicately branched stems of small, irregular flowers having 2 sepals, 4 united petals (forming a spur), 6 stamens, and 1 ovary. Most leaves are basal and are finely dissected. The stems are very soft and watery.

(11) Evening Primrose / Onagraceae---herbaceous plants having spikes of showy flowers with 4 sepals, 4 petals, and an ovary seen distinctly as a branched stigma. Leaves are simple and on the stems, arising from deep horizontal roots.

(12) Figwort or Snapdragon / Scrophulariaceae---herbaceous plants with spikes or racemes or many irregularly shaped flowers having 5 united sepals, 5 united petals, 4 (sometimes 2) stamens, and 1 ovary. Most leaves are simple, except for pedicularis, which is pinnately divided with a broad mid-rib.

(13) Gentian / Gentianaceae---herbaceous plants with tubular or salverform flowers having 4 or 5 sepals (sometimes united), 4 or 5 united petals, 4 or 5 stamens, and 1 obviously protruding ovary. Leaves are entire, simple and usually opposite on the stout stems.

(14) Geranium / Geraniaceae---herbaceous plants having branched stems of large flowers with 5 sepals, 5 clawed petals, 10 stamens, and a 5-parted extruded ovary that resembles a crane's bill. Alaska members have long-stemmed, palmately-divided leaves, mostly basal.

(15) Gooseberry / Grossulariaceae---shrubs sometimes with thorns, having small flowers with 4 or 5 sepals, 5 very small inconspicuous petals, 5 stamens, and a 2-parted ovary in the form of a berry. Leaves are usually lobed with teeth.

(16) Goosefoot / Chenopodiaceae---herbaceous plants with spikes of small, mostly green, inconspicuous clusters of flowers with 5 sepals, no petals, 5 stamens, and 1 ovary. These are mostly weedy plants usually with opposite leaves.

(17) Heath / Ericaceae---mostly shrubs, frequently evergreen, with bell or urn or cup-shaped flowers. Flowers have 4 or 5 (sometimes united) sepals, 4 or 5 (usually united) petals, 4 or 5 stamens, and 1 ovary. The leaves are entire, simple and, usually narrow. Usually found in acidic soil.

(18) Honeysuckle / Caprifoliaceae---shrubs with tubular or salverform flowers having 5 sepals, 5 united petals, 5 stamens, and 1 ovary. Leaves are toothed and opposite.

(19) Lily / Liliaceae---frequently bulbous plants usually with a stout flower stalk. Flowers have 6 tepals (3 sepals, 3 petals), 6 stamens, and a 3-parted ovary. Flowers are in a raceme or umbel. Leaves have parallel veins and, frequently, clasp the stem.

(20) Mustard / Brassicaceae---herbaceous plants with branched inflorescences of flowers having 4 sepals, 4 petals, 6 stamens (4 high and 2 low), and 1 ovary. Leaves are mostly basal, but frequently continue up the flower stalk. Distinct seed stalk as silicle or silique. Most members have edible leaves.

(21) Madder / Rubiaceae---herbaceous plants having a panicle of small salverform flowers with 4 sepals, 4 united petals, 4 stamens, and 1 2-parted ovary. Some varieties have square stems, all have entire leaves that are opposite or in a whorl.

(22) Moschatel / Adoxaceae---herbaceous plants. There is one small member in Alaska having one 4-petalled flower at the end of the stem and four 5-petalled flowers surrounding it. The basal leaves are thin, yellowish-green with broad, toothed lobes. Blooms very early and is very small.

(23) Oleaster / Elaegnaceae---shrubs having salverform flowers with 4 sepals, no petals, 4 stamens, and 1 ovary in the form of a berry. Leaves are simple, entire, and have scales.

(24) Orchid / Orchidaceae---herbaceous plants with irregularly shaped flowers having 3 sepals, 3 petals (the lower are ''saclike''). Flower stalks are stout, leaves usually alternate (sometimes opposite), simple with parallel veins (monocot).

(25) Parsley / Apiaceae---herbaceous plants with umbels of small flowers having 5 sepals, 5 petals, 5 stamens, and a 2-parted ovary. Most leaves are pinnately divided and finely dissected or toothed. Many plants have hollow stems and leaves with petioles that clasp the stems.

(26) Pea / Fabaceae---herbaceous plants having irregular flowers, with 5 united sepals, 5 petals (the lower 2 joined to form a keel), 10 stamens, and 1 pistil. Leaves are entire, pinnately divided, often with stipules, sometimes with tendrils.

(27) Phlox / Polemoniaceae---herbaceous plants having flowers with 5 united sepals, 5 rounded united petals, 5 stamens and a 3-parted ovary. Leaves are entire and can be simple or pinnately divided.

(28) Pink / Caryophyllaceae---herbaceous plants with 5 sepals, 5 rounded united petals, 10 stamens, and a 5-parted ovary. The entire, simple leaves are placed opposite on the stems which are swollen at the joints.

(29) Poppy / Papaveraceae---herbaceous plants having flowers with 2 deciduous sepals, 4 large petals, many stamens, and a large, many-seeded ovary. The leaves having petioles are mostly basal, hairy, and pinnately divided.

(30) Primrose / Primulaceae---herbaceous plants with flowers having 5 sepals, 5 united petals, 5 stamens, and a 5-parted ovary. Leaves are mostly basal, and, usually, glabrous.

(31) Purslane / Portulacaceae---herbaceous plants with flowers having 2 sepals, 5 petals and usually 5 stamens. These are small plants with smooth, entire, spatulate basal leaves. Usually found in damp areas.

(32) Rose / Rosaceae---plants or shrubs with flowers having 5 sepals, usually 5 petals, many stamens, and one to many fruits. Leaves are varied, but most are pinnately divided and have stipules.

(33) Sandlewood / Santalaceae---plants, sometimes parasitic, with 3 to 5 sepals and no petals. Leaves are usually simple and alternate.

(34) Saxifrage / Saxifragaceae---plants usually with mostly simple basal leaves and reduced, alternate stem leaves. Flowers usually have 5 sepals, 5 petals, 10 stamens. Some genera have a pronounced (often cone-shaped) ovary. Most have a single ovary with two carpels joined at the base.

(35) Stonecrop, Sedum / Crassulaceae---small succulent plants with many thick, succulent, stalkless, undivided, stem leaves. Flowers have 4 or 5 sepals, 4 or 5 petals, and 8 or 10 stamens.

(36) Valerian / Valerianaceae---plants with opposite stem leaves and sometimes long-stemmed basal leaves. Flowers have 5 joined petals and are bell-shaped or salverform.

(37) Violet / Violaceae---small plants with long-stemmed, heart-shaped leaves. Flowers are irregular, have 5 sepals, 5 petals, and a spur.

(38) Wintergreen / Pyrolaceae---small plants with simple, petiolate, evergreen leaves. Flowers are usually on a heavy stalk, often showing the color of the flowers. The flowers have 5 sepals, 5 somewhat waxy petals, 10 stamens, and a 5-parted ovary with a protruding style.

GLOSSARY

Acute: Sharply pointed.

Aggregate: In reference to fruit type. Separate carpels grouped together to form a fruit. Examples: Raspberry and cloudberry.

Alpine: Growing above timberline.

Alternate: Leaf or branch arrangement on stem, not opposite each other.

Annual: A plant growing from seed, blooming, setting seed and then dying all in one growing season.

Aquatic: Living in the water.

Arcuate: Usually referring to veins of a leaf that are bowed or follow the curve of the leaf and appear to be nearly parallel.

Axil: The upper angle formed by the junction of a main stem and a leaf stalk or branch.

Barbellate: Having barbs, sharp points, bristles. Usually reflexed.

Basal: Situated at, or pertaining to, the base.

Beak: An obvious, elongated or pointed, end of a plant part.

Bearded: A line or tuft of hairs.

Berry: A soft, fleshy, multi-seeded fruit.

Bi-pinnately divided: Describing a pinnate leaf in which the leaflets are further divided in a pinnate fashion.

Biennial: Of two seasons duration from seed to maturity and death.

Binomial: The botanical nomenclature, or scientific name of a plant; consisting of the genus name and the species name.

Blade: The expanded part of a leaf, petal or sepal.

Bloom: A whitish coating on a fruit that, usually, can be rubbed off. Often waxy looking.

Bog: A low, very wet area. Soil is often acidic, and standing water is common.

Bract: A reduced or modified leaf, usually below a flower, often petal-like.

Bracteoles: A small bract on top of a pedicel instead of below it.

Bristles: Long, stiff hairs.

Bulb: A structure below the surface of the ground, consisting of overlapping leaf bases. Like an onion. Common in the lily family.

Bulbous: Growing from a bulb-like structure.

Calyx: The outermost circle of the floral parts. The external portion, usually green. The group of sepals.

Campanulate: Bell-shaped.

Capitate: Having a dense, head-like cluster.

Capsule: A dry fruit composed of more than 1 seed cavity.

Carpel: The structure of the plant that holds the seeds.

Catkin: A tight spike of petal-less flowers (usually either male or female).

Caudex: The woody base of a perennial plant.

Channeled: Having a groove or lengthwise depression.

Ciliate: Having hairs along the edges.

Clasping: Partially surrounding the stem (usually referring to a leaf petiole).

Clawed: Narrow, stalk-like base of some petals or sepals.

Clone: A plant reproduced vegetatively, making it identical to the parent plant.

Cluster: A tight grouping, or bunch.

Colonizer: Establishing a new or disturbed area. Usually done by plants that like sun light and can survive in shallow soil with few nutrients.

Conical: Cone-shaped, having a pointed top.

Cuneate: Wedge-shaped, narrowing at the base.

Cylindrical: In the shape of a cylinder, column or tube.

Cyme: A flat-topped flower cluster, with central flowers opening first.

Deciduous: Not persistent, said of leaves falling in autumn or of floral parts falling after flowering.

Decumbent: Sprawling on the ground with upturned ends.

Dentate: Having a margin or edge cut with sharp teeth directed outward.

Diamond Willow: A common name given to several willows that produce diamond-like depressions on their trunks. These are the result of a fungus that attacks the place where a branch has broken off from the main trunk. This usually occurs in areas that stay wet most of the time.

Dissected: Cut or divided into sections.

Drupe: A fleshy fruit having one seed inside a tough shell.

Elliptical: Mostly oval, tapering to both ends equally.

Entire: Without divisions, lobes, or teeth. With even or smooth margin or edge.

Epipetalous: Referring to stamens that are attached on the petals, not at the base of them.

Ethnic: Pertaining to a person, or group of people, who are native to, or have tradition ally lived in, an area.

Evergreen: Remaining green all year.

Extruded: Pushed out. Extending beyond normal range.

Fall: A term for the large, petal-like sepals of the Iris family.

Farinose: Covered with a powdery substance.

Fascicle: A tight bundle, cluster or clump.

Fibrous: Usually referring to roots. Most being the same size. None being dormant. Common with monocots.

Fleshy: Soft or puffy.

Frond: Leaf of a fern. (Also, a large leaf).

Genus: A group of closely related plants. The first part of a binomial or scientific name.

Glabrous: Having a smooth, even surface without hairs.

Glandular: Having a substance (often sticky) that is released from the plant by way of pores or hairs.

Glaucous: Having a waxy, grayish-blue appearance.

Globular: Round.

Heath: Open wasteland, usually having acidic soil.

Herbaceous: A non-woody, perennial plant, with above ground parts dying to the ground each year.

Hummock: A rounded rise of vegetation Usually in a wet area; such as, a bog or marsh.

Hybrid: A cross between 2 species or subspecies, usually of the same genus.

Incisions: Sharp cuts or indentations, usually referring to leaf edges.

Inflorescence: A flower cluster, or grouping on a stem.

Insectivorous: Referring to plants that capture insects, and absorb nutrients from them.

Introduced: Said of plants that were not originally native to an area, becoming established after escaping from farmlands or in reseeding projects.

Involucre: A group of bracts beneath a flower cluster, as in the heads of the aster family.

Lanceolate: Narrow, tapering to both ends.

Lateral: Situated to the side.

Leaflet: A single part of a compound leaf.

Linear: Long and narrow, usually having mostly parallel edges.

Lobed: Describing a leaf that is divided into curved or rounded parts connected to each other by an undivided central area.

Lyrate: Lyre shaped. A pinnatifid leaf with a larger end lobe, like a dandelion leaf.

Margin: Edge.

Meadow: A moist, open area, usually free of shrubs and trees.

Monocot: A plant arising from a seed bearing one leaf. The monocot families that are included in this book are: Grass, sedge, rush, lily and orchid. Plants usually have leaves with parallel veins and flower parts in multiples of three.

Native Plant: Any plant that grows naturally in the area of concern, not placed there in either plant or seed form.

Nectaries: A structure giving off a sweet substance, usually sticky.

Nerve: An unbranched vein or narrow ridge.

Node: A joint of a stolon or stem, or the point on a stem where the leaf begins.

Nomenclature: The scientific naming of plants.

Nut: A dry, hard, one-seeded fruit.

Nutlet: A small nut.

Oblanceolate: Similar to lanceolate, but broader at base.

Oblong: Much longer than broad, with nearly parallel margins and a rounded tip.

Opaque: Not letting light through, not transparent nor translucent.

Ovary: The lower swollen portion of the reproductive part of a plant, containing the seeds.

Ovate: Egg-shaped, with a point.

Ovoid: Egg-shaped.

Palmate: Lobed, divided or ribbed so as to resemble the outstretched fingers of a hand.

Pappus: Bristles, hairs, etc. In the Aster family, attached to the seed.

Parasitic: An organism obtaining food and/or shelter at the expense of another.

Pedicel: The stalk attaching individual flowers to the main stem of the inflorescence.

Perennial: Living for more than two years; and, usually, flowering each year after the first.

Persistent: Remaining on a plant after other vegetative parts have fallen off.

Petal: Usually the colorful part of the corolla, the row of floral parts within the sepals.

Petiolate: Having a petiole.

Petiole: The stalk that attaches the leaf to the stem.

Pinnate: Describing a compound leaf in which the leaflets are arranged in two rows, one on each side of the midrib.

Pinnatifid: Divided in a pinnate fashion.

Pistil: A term used ambiguously to describe either a single carpel (simple pistil) or a group of fused carpels (compound pistil).

Pistillate: A flower that has only the female reproductive parts.

Prickle: A short woody pointed outgrowth from the epidermis of a plant.

Raceme: An inflorescence in which the flowers are formed on individual pedicels attached to the main stem.

Ray Flower: The flat outer flowers of the aster family, often incorrectly referred to as petals of a daisy.

Reflexed: Bent abruptly downward or backward.

Revegetate: To plant again, usually an attempt to restore to original and/or acceptable condition.

Rhizome: An underground stem or rootstock, usually rooting at the nodes, becoming upcurved at the end.

Rosette: A crowded cluster of leaves, appearing to rise from one point in the ground.

Runner: A stolon or trailing stem.

Sac-like: Having a swollen pouch.

Saline: Containing salt.

Salverform: A tube-shaped flower, with petals that flatten out at right angles from the tube.

Scale: A dry leaf, or bract, usually beneath the flowering parts of a plant.

Scientific Name (Botanical Name): Often derived from Greek or Latin, and consisting of two parts. The first part being the genus name, and the second part being the species or specific name, which describes a plant characteristic or after an early explorer or naturalist.

Scree: Fine rock and gravel on steep slopes, often sliding with heavy rain and snow, supporting scattered vegetation.

Sepal: One of the outer group of floral parts. Usually green .

Serrated: Having sharply pointed teeth or indentations.

Sessile: Without a stalk or stem.

Sheath: A tubular (often thin) plant structure that surrounds a plant part. Often at a connection where a petiole meets the stem. Typical of many members of the parsley family.

Shrub: A woody perennial, smaller than a tree, usually with several basal stems.

Silicle: The seed capsule of some members of the mustard family, usually no more than twice as long as wide.

Silique: The seed capsule of many members of the mustard family, more than twice as long as wide.

Simple: Not branched or divided.

Sinus: An indentation or depression between 2 lobes of a leaf, or where the leaf meets the petiole.

Spadix: A thick fleshy stem (like a spike) that bears many flowers and fruits of a plant.

Spathe: A large bract, or pair of bracts, often petal-like, enclosing a flower cluster or spadix.

Spatulate: Describing structures that have a broad end and a long narrow base, such as the leaves of the daisy.

Species: A further division of plants beyond genus, showing slight differences. More specifically, the specific epithet, or second part of the binomial or scientific name.

Spike: An inflorescence like a raceme, but without individual flower stems.

Spine: The stiff mid-portion of a leaf, or a long pointed end or thorn.

Spore: The small, dust-like, asexual, unicellular reproductive body of flowerless plants.

Spur: A tubular or sac-like part of a flower. It usually contains a nectar secreting gland.

Stamen: The male organ of the flower, consisting of a filament and an anther, the latter bearing the pollen.

Staminate: A flower that has only the male reproductive part.

Stellate: Star-shaped.

Stigma: The top part of a pistil or style, often hairy and/or sticky, which receives the pollen at pollination time and on which the pollen grain germinates.

Stigmatic Rays: Ridges on the top of a seed capsule, radiating from the center, as in the poppy family.

Stipe: The stalk beneath the ovary. The leaf stalk of a fern.

Stipule: A part of the leaf where it attaches to the stem (especially common in the rose and pea families). A broadening on either side of the stem that could be mistaken for a bract.

Stolons: Runners or trailing stems.

Stomata (singular stoma): Small openings or pores in the surface of a leaf through which gaseous exchange takes place between the internal tissues and the atmosphere.

Style: The tubular part of the reproductive portion of a plant that connects the stigma to the ovary.

Sub-shrub: A very low shrub.

Succulent: Fleshy, juicy.

Talus: An accumulation of large and medium size pieces of rock that have broken off from cliffs above. Very little vegetation grows there, except on the perimeters, due to lack of soil and humus material.

Tap Root: A long, usually thick, root which allows a plant to store energy and reach deep in the soil for water and nutrients. Plants with tap root usually grow in dry or rocky areas. A tap root also helps to anchor a plant in unstable soil.

Teeth: Notches along the margins of leaves.

Tendril: A long thread-like part of a plant stem that supports it by twining around other objects. Notable in members of the pea family.

Terminal: At the end.

Thicket: A dense growth of bushes or shrub-like trees. In Denali Park, often an area between tundra and treeline.

Toxin: A soluble toxic product of a bacterial cell which is capable of diffusing out of the living cell into the surrounding medium.

Transluscent: Allowing some light through without being able to see inside.

Treeline: The elevation above which trees no longer grow. In Denali Park, usually between 2500 and 3000 feet.

Tubular: Having the form of, or consisting of, a tube or tubes.

Tufted: Clustered, clumped, having a bunch of hairs, leaves or stems arising from the same point.

Tundra: Treeless arctic plain, often times damp and having mounds.

Tundra: Treeless land, often rocks intermixed with plants. Can be wet or dry.

Umbel: An inflorescence, rounded to flat-topped, in which all of the pedicels arise at the same point, like the ribs of an umbrella.

Unisexual: A single sex plant. One that bears only stamens or carpels, not both.

Vegetative Reproduction: A) Reproduction by divisions or sections of plants, or B) by roots, stolons or runners.

Waste Places: Areas where soil has been stripped of its naturally occurring vegetation. Usually lack of humus, soil and care causes it to develop into a different environment and plant community than it was originally. Generally referring to roadside pull-offs, old roadbeds, around old buildings and townsites.

Watery: Juicy. Said of plants with a non-fibrous stem.

Whorl: An arrangement of leaves, etc., in a circle around the stem, radiating from a node. Three or more leaves or flowers at one node, in a circle.

Wing: A) In reference to flowers, the lateral (side) petals of members of the pea family, B) In reference to seeds, a dry, thin portion extending around the edge, usually for the purpose of spreading the seed by wind action.

COROLLA OR FLOWER PARTS

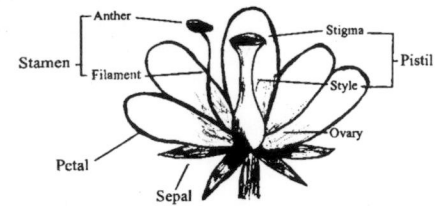

INFLORESCENCES

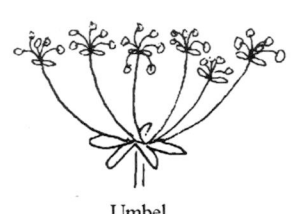 

Umbel   Spike

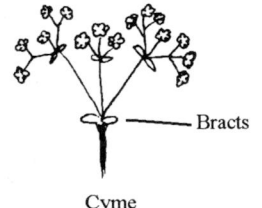 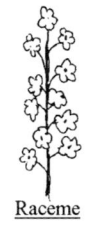

Bracts

Cyme   Raceme

Corymb   Panicle

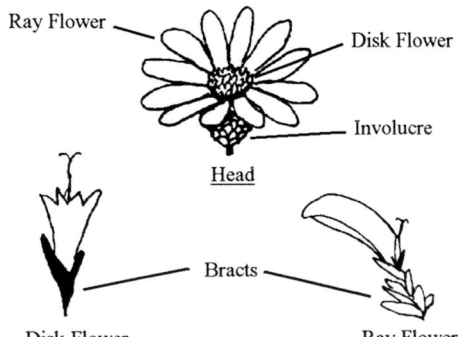

Ray Flower   Disk Flower

Involucre

Head

Bracts

Disk Flower   Ray Flower

COROLLA (FLOWER) TYPES

Campanulate   Bell

Funnel   Urn

Tube   Salverform

Regular or Symmetrical   Irregular

Labiate   Spurred

Papilionaceous

LEAF ARRANGEMENT

Alternate   Opposite

Basal   Whorled

LEAF SHAPES

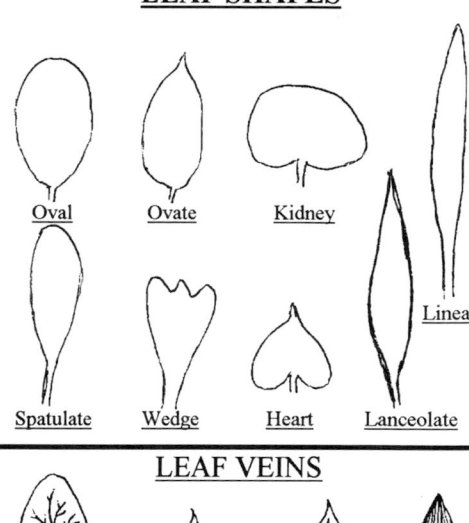

Oval   Ovate   Kidney

Linear

Spatulate   Wedge   Heart   Lanceolate

SIMPLE LEAVES

LEAF VEINS

Pinnate   Palmate   Arcuate   Parallel

COMPOUND LEAVES

Pinnate   Pallmate

LEAF EDGES

Entire   Toothed   Lobed   Laciniate

Ciliate   Dissected

GROWTH METHODS

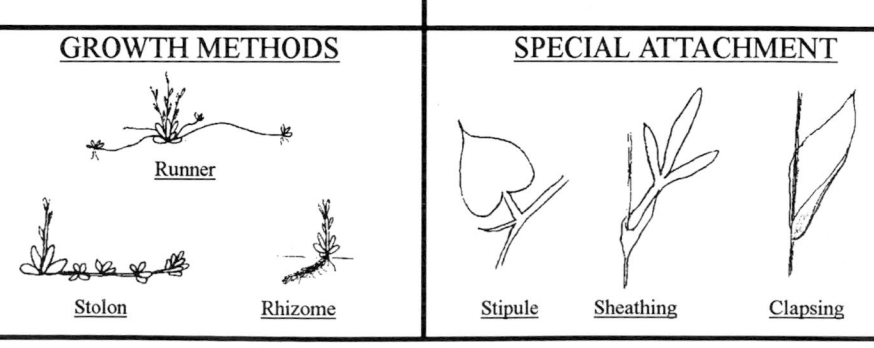

Runner

Stolon   Rhizome

SPECIAL ATTACHMENT

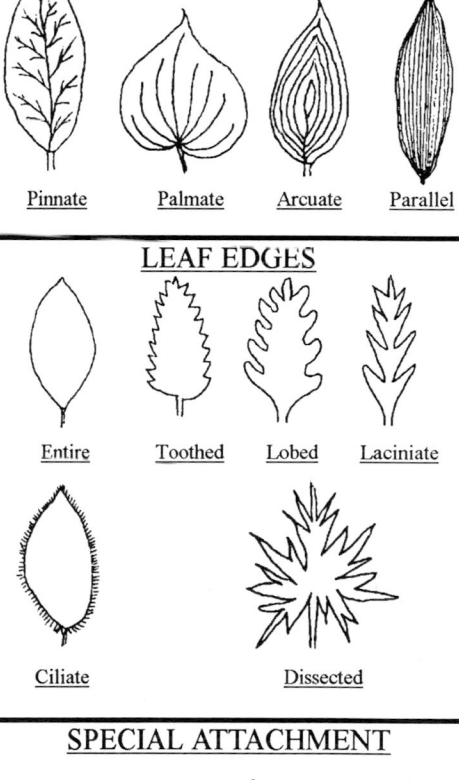

Stipule   Sheathing   Clapsing

BIBLIOGRAPHY

Croner, Don. 1989. **15 Hikes in Denali National Park.** Transalaska Publishing Co. 42 pp.

Penny Rennick, General Editor. 1988. **Denali.** Alaska Geographic Society. 95 pp.

Forbes, Sheri. 1992. **The Nature of Denali.** Alaska Natural History Association. 42 pp.

Heacox, Kim. 1986. **The Denali Road Guide.** Alaska Natural History Association. 48 pp.

Heller, Christine. 1953. **Wild Edible and Poisonous Plants of Alaska.** Univ. Alaska Ext. Bull. F-40. 87 pp.

Hultén, Eric. 1968. **Flora of Alaska and Neighboring Territories.** Stanford University Press. 1008 pp.

Hultén, Eric. 1973. **Supplement to Flora of Alaska and Neighboring Territories.** Swedish Museum of Natural History. 512 pp.

Montague, Richard W. 1973. **Exploring Mt. McKinley National Park.** Alaska Travel Publications. 293 pp.

Smith, James P., Jr. 1977. **Vascular Plant Families.** Mad River Press, Eureka, California. 321 pp.

Viereck, Leslie A., and Little, Elbert L., Jr. 1972. **Alaska Trees and Shrubs.** Forest Service, U. S. Dept. of Agriculture. Washington, D. C. 266 pp.

Welsh, Stanley L. 1974. **Anderson's Flora of Alaska and Adjacent Parts of Canada.** Brigham Young University Press, Provo, Utah. 724 pp.

Index

W

Y

Z